This book is about happiness—how to achieve it. Read it prayerfully; implement its teachings into your own life, and I guarantee the end result will be happiness.

From the Foreword by
TIM LAHAYE

BILL BRIGHT'S
"THE JOY OF KNOWING GOD"
SERIES

1. *THE JOY OF TRUSTING GOD*

2. *THE JOY OF FINDING JESUS*

3. *THE JOY OF SPIRIT-FILLED LIVING*

4. *THE JOY OF INTIMACY WITH GOD*

5. *THE JOY OF TOTAL FORGIVENESS*

6. *THE JOY OF ACTIVE PRAYER*

7. *THE JOY OF FAITHFUL OBEDIENCE*

8. *THE JOY OF SUPERNATURAL THINKING*

9. *THE JOY OF DYNAMIC GIVING*

10. *THE JOY OF SHARING JESUS*

the JOY of FAITHFUL OBEDIENCE

DR. BILL BRIGHT

The Bible Teacher's Teacher

COOK COMMUNICATIONS MINISTRIES
Colorado Springs, Colorado • Paris, Ontario
KINGSWAY COMMUNICATIONS LTD
Eastbourne, England

Victor® is an imprint of
Cook Communications Ministries,
Colorado Springs, CO 80918
Cook Communications, Paris, Ontario
Kingsway Communications, Eastbourne, England

THE JOY OF FAITHFUL OBEDIENCE
© 2005 by Bright Media Group

First Printing, 2005
Printed in United States of America
1 2 3 4 5 6 7 8 9 10 Printing/Year 09 08 07 06 05

Cover Design: Brand Navigation, LLC

Library of Congress Cataloging-in-Publication Data

Bright, Bill.
   The joy of faithful obedience : your way to God's best / Bill Bright.
      p. cm. -- (The joy of knowing God series ; bk. 7)
   ISBN 0-7814-4252-4 (pbk.)
   1. Ten commandments. I. Title. II. Series.

BV4655.B67 2005
241.5'2--dc22

                        2004027061

Dedication

GLOBAL FOUNDING PARTNERS

The Bright Media Foundation continues the multifaceted ministries of Bill and Vonette Bright for generations yet unborn. God has touched and inspired the Brights through the ministries of writers through the centuries. Likewise, they wish to pass along God's message in Jesus Christ as they have experienced it, seeking to inspire, train, and transform lives, thereby helping to fulfill the Great Commission each year until our Lord returns.

Many generous friends have prayed and sacrificed to support the Bright Media Foundation's culturally relevant, creative works, in print and electronic forms. The following persons specifically have helped to establish the foundation. These special friends will always be known as Global Founding Partners *of the Bright Media Foundation.*

Bill and Christie Heavener and family

Stuart and Debra Sue Irby and family

Edward E. Haddock Jr., Edye Murphy-Haddock, and the Haddock family

Acknowledgments

It was my privilege to share fifty-four years, six months, and twenty days of married life with a man who loved Jesus passionately and served Him faithfully. Six months before his home going, Bill initiated what has become "The Joy of Knowing God" series. It was his desire to pass along to future generations the insights God had given him that they, too, could discover God's magnificence and live out the wonderful plan He has for their lives.

"The Joy of Knowing God" series is a collection of Bill Bright's top ten life-changing messages. Millions of people around the world have already benefited greatly from these spiritual truths and are now living the exciting Christian adventure that God desires for each of us.

On behalf of Bill, I want to thank the following team that helped research, compile, edit, and wordsmith the manuscripts and audio scripts in this series: Jim Bramlett, Rebecca Cotton, Eric Metaxas, Sheryl Moon, Cecil Price, Michael Richardson, Eric Stanford, and Rob Suggs.

I also want to thank Bill's longtime friends and Campus Crusade associates Bailey Marks and Ted Martin, who carefully reviewed the scripts and manuscripts for accuracy.

Bill was deeply grateful to Bob Angelotti and Don Stillman of Allegiant Marketing Group for their encouragement to produce this series and their ingenuity in facilitating distribution to so many.

A special thanks to Cook Communications and its team of dedicated professionals who partnered with Bright Media Foundation in this venture, as well as to Steve Laube, who brought us together.

Last but not least, I want to express my appreciation to Helmut Teichert, who worked faithfully and diligently in overseeing this team that Bill's vision would be realized, and to John Nill, CEO of Bright Media, who has helped me navigate the many challenges along this journey.

As a result of the hard work of so many, and especially our wonderful Lord's promise of His grace, I trust that multitudes worldwide will experience a greater joy by knowing God and His ways more fully.

With a grateful heart,
MRS. BILL BRIGHT (VONETTE)

Contents

Foreword by Tim LaHaye 9

1. Find True Happiness 13

2. God's Law Leads to Christ's Grace...........23

3. Commandment #1 Keep God
   Above All Else 33

4. Commandment #2 Shun Idols......................41

5. Commandment #3 Revere the
   Lord's Name..49

6. Commandment #4 Respect the
   Lord's Day..57

7. Commandment #5 Honor Your Parents.....67

8. Commandment #6 Value Human Life........77

9. Commandment #7 Have a Right
   View of Sex 87

10. Commandment #8 Respect What Belongs
    to Others 97

11. Commandment #9 Tell the Truth............107

12. Commandment #10 Be Satisfied with
    What You Have..111

13. Live It! 121

Readers' Guide 130

Appendix: God's Word on
Faithful Obedience 139

Foreword

When I started reading the manuscript for this book, I expected it to be a good read; after all, my friend of more than forty-five years, Bill Bright, was the author, and he already had several good books in print. Besides, the subject is one I am highly interested in and on which I have even thought of writing myself. But frankly, I was not prepared to find this title such an incredibly interesting and helpful book dealing with one of the most important issues of our day—how modern Christians relate to the Ten Commandments.

I had forgotten what a great storyteller Bill is. This book is filled with some of the most interesting stories you have ever read, and each one illustrates an important point. I also admire his courage in dealing carefully with some almost-forgotten issues in today's church. Our Lord said, "If you love Me, keep My commandments," yet few Christians even know them all or could recite them. In fact, I don't think many Christians even know where to look in the Bible to find them.

Yet our very happiness is dependent on keeping His commands. Our Lord said, "Blessed [or happy] are they who hear the word of God and keep it." The psalmist has said, "Blessed are those who walk in the law of the Lord." By contrast, miserable are those who do not. As a pastor-counselor for many years, I have observed that everyone who came to me for help was miserable. My wife used to kid me and say, "It's your personality. You naturally draw miserable people to you." Actually, happy people never go to their pastor or a counselor and say,

"I'm so happy I just can't stand it so I came to you for help." No, it is miserable people who seek out counseling.

Then I began to notice a pattern in the stories these unhappy people told. They had violated one or more of the laws or principles of God. In short, they had earned a right to be miserable by violating His laws. It didn't matter that they didn't obey them because they didn't know them; they were still miserable.

That is when I developed the understanding that God meant His commands, precepts, and admonitions for our good. After that I looked on my role as a counselor as that of a listener to discern what commands of God the individuals were violating. Then I would graciously confront them with the Word of God so they could seek His help in changing their behavior. The end result is happiness.

Everyone wants to be happy. It's natural. But few people realize that happiness does not just happen; it is the result of obeying the commands, precepts, and principles of God. That is what they are for. Jesus said it best: "If you know these things [the principles of God], happy are you *if* you do them!" This book will help you realize how very important God's commandments are and how practical they are in our modern era, and will offer many suggestions on how to obey them.

Bill Bright was one of the most productive soul winners and encouragers of other Christians to serve their Lord in the last century. He walked with God and kept His commandments for more than fifty years. No wonder he was one of the happiest and fulfilled men in our generation! He was seeking in this well-written book to share his happiness.

This book is about happiness—how to achieve it. Read it

prayerfully, implement its teachings into your own life, and I guarantee the end result will be happiness. Actually, *I* can't guarantee anything. Your guarantee of happiness is based on the Word of God, including the words of Jesus in Revelation 22:13–14: "'I am the Alpha and the Omega, the Beginning and the End, the First and the Last.' Blessed are those who do His commandments …" (NKJV).

—TIM LAHAYE

———————◆———————

"'You must love the Lord your God with all your heart, all your soul, and all your mind.' This is the first and greatest commandment."

—Jesus Christ

———————————————

1

Find True Happiness

Have you ever wondered, "How does a person find true happiness?"

In one way or another, many of us have contemplated, wrestled with, or puzzled over this question at some point in our lives. It is the fundamental quest of humanity, but sadly, most people never find the answer. However, after fifty years of ministry and an incredible life of adventure with Jesus Christ as my Savior, I can tell you with certainty and great enthusiasm—obeying God and His Laws is the way to find true happiness! Nothing in this world can match the joy and satisfaction of honoring and serving God by obeying his commands.

But this joy comes from more than just following a list of rules. It comes from loving God. And love for God results in obedience. Therefore, successfully obeying God's Laws begins with one simple principle. Jesus said, "'You must love the Lord your God with all your heart, all your soul, and all your mind.' This is the first and greatest commandment" (Matthew 22:37–38). These verses explain true happiness in a nutshell. There is no other way to experience the kind of joy that remains through hard times and good times, through moun-taintop highs and valley lows, in days of plenty and days of need. All of God's commandments are wrapped up in this one great commandment.

God Wants the Good Life for You

God gave us the Ten Commandments to bring joy and hap-piness to every part of our lives. The Ten Commandments communicate the essence of how we must relate to God and to our fellow man.

But perhaps you are thinking, *This is too hard to do. I could never obtain the perfection that the Ten Commandments demand.*

The Ten Commandments, simple and profound as they are, are impossible for any of us to keep. We are imperfect humans who hopelessly fail to live up to God's standards in our own self-effort.

Only as we rely on God's power can we truly attain the standard that God sets for our behavior. When we observe the Ten Commandments in the power of God's Spirit, they liberate us so we can experience the joy of pleasing God. They guide us along the path He has planned for our lives, and they protect us from wrongdoing and its consequences. God's commandments unlock the blessings He has in store for us.

> *The fact is, law and grace are absolutely, beautifully intertwined.*

God's Gift to You

God gave us the Ten Commandments not to ensure the absence of evil but to ensure the presence of purity.

Although God intended the Ten Commandments to provide rules for living, they are much more than a simple set of do's and don'ts.

God gave them to us as a special gift. The Ten Commandments deserve the highest place of honor and distinction in our lives. This is demonstrated by the special place that they occupied when God first gave them to the Jewish people. Before the nation of Israel could hear God's Law at Mount Sinai, they first had to prepare themselves through ceremonial cleansing. From this we learn that nothing unclean can dwell in the presence of a holy God. Furthermore, Mount Sinai, where God appeared to Moses, was to be off-limits. No one was permitted to approach the holy mount where God was. God's Law was no ordinary gift.

God did not bother dictating His commandments to Moses for him to record. God was His own secretary! The very finger of God wrote the commandments on tablets made of stone. This fact distinguishes the Ten Commandments from all other books of the Bible, which were given to men by inspiration of the Holy Spirit. Although the entire Bible is God's inspired Word, the Ten Commandments stand as God's *personal,* inscribed Word to man.

God also spoke these commands to Moses in an audible voice. Can you imagine the scene? The mighty voice of God declaring His will for man atop a smoke-filled mountain with peals of thunder and lightning filling the sky. I marvel at the very thought of it.

After Moses brought the tablets down from the mountain, they were placed inside the Ark of the Covenant. The Ark was a rectangular chest made of special wood covered with gold. On top of the Ark was the mercy seat. It was made of pure gold and was held in place by a golden ridge or crown. Beaten out of the same piece of pure gold as the mercy seat were two cherubim with their wings overshadowing the Ark. The Ark of the Covenant was undoubtedly a very beautiful and expensive piece of furniture. And it was built to house the Ten Commandments.

Later, Solomon's temple was built as a home for the Ark. It has been estimated that to construct Solomon's temple and the Ark of the Covenant today would cost $2 billion! The inner sanctuary and altar of Solomon's temple were overlaid with gold. Even the floor was covered with gold. God wanted the commandments to be housed in a place of beauty and majesty. It is important for us to understand that God ascribes a great deal of value to His Law.

Why did God give the Ten Commandments to the people of Israel? Because He loved them. The awesome display of God's mighty power at Mount Sinai and the beauty of the temple remind us that the Ten Commandments are ten ways God says, "I love you."

Why, then, do we need the Ten Commandments today? From having no other gods before Him to not desiring things that are not ours to possess, the Ten Commandments serve as God's divine gauge to help us discover peace and blessing for our lives.

People often ask, "If I'm under grace, do the Ten Commandments still apply to me?" The Ten Commandments are timeless. They are absolutely as important today as when Moses delivered them millenniums ago.

Yet today a relativistic mind-set toward biblically based morality is sweeping every area of society. A Barna Research Group survey asked, "Is there absolute truth?" Amazingly, 66 percent of American adults responded that they believe that "there is no such thing as absolute truth; different people can define truth in conflicting ways and still be correct."

The Ten Commandments stand as a towering refutation to those who believe there is no truth. The commandments contain the essence of God's unchangeable and absolute

—————❖—————

"Love the Lord your God with all your heart, all your soul, and all your mind" ... true happiness in a nutshell.

—————————

truth. When we follow the Ten Commandments, we benefit because they do more than steer us in the right direction, they also keep us from taking the wrong path. They set the boundaries that protect us from the quicksand we surely will encounter in life. Without righteous law, we live without direction.

A REMINDER OF GOD'S GRACE

Society today is dominated by overworked and overburdened people who struggle each day with a world of concerns. We work to provide for our families, pay a never-ending mound of bills, raise children, and do a list of other things that challenge us to keep it all together. Add to this our church, which looks for our time and energy, and our children, who anticipate that we will have all the answers to life. Soon the pressures seem insurmountable. But perhaps our greatest sense of spiritual pressure comes from the burden we often feel when we are not dealing effectively with sin.

Perhaps you are feeling, "I am already overwhelmed and feel like I am not living the way I should, and now you want to lay the Ten Commandments on me?" The Ten Commandments can actually aid you in finding peace in the midst of your stressed existence!

How does this work? To understand, we have to first know how it doesn't work. The Bible is clear that no one can earn God's blessing through a life of toil and good works. When we read through the Ten Commandments, it doesn't take long to realize that we have failed to live up to God's perfect standards. We know there have been occasions when we have not given God first place in our lives, when we have failed to honor our father and mother, we've violated the Sabbath, we've lied, we've looked at another person with lust in our hearts, or we've desired something that belonged to someone else. Whatever our wrongdoings, our lives are proof to the testimony of the Scripture that insists "all have sinned; all fall short of God's glorious standard" (Romans 3:23).

> ❖
>
> *The Ten Commandments are ten ways God says, "I love you."*

When I think about my failure to live according to God's perfect law, I am driven to the truth of the cross of Jesus Christ and His incredible work of salvation on my behalf. I am reminded of my own sinfulness.

The sad truth is that the gospel of Jesus is not only a message of love and forgiveness; it is also an indictment of our sinfulness. The cross of Jesus Christ is God's opinion of us. It says that our sins are an affront to Him. Without the mercy of God poured out at Calvary, we would be the ones suffering the full penalty for our sins—a penalty brought about by our failure to comply with God's holy standards. It is our spiritual poverty in light of these facts that drives us to a greater sense of our need for God's divine grace.

Because the Law reveals our inability to be what God has called us to be, we can admit our failure, be filled with His

Holy Spirit, and live His commandments with joy and confidence. Then all our service will be accomplished for God out of a heart of love and joyful gratitude for what Christ has done for us and not from our own human resolve, which produces frustration and defeat. With the Holy Spirit's help, we will find the strength we need to live a life of fruitful abundance, even in the midst of the strongest opposition.

I firmly believe that seeking approval from God and others through performance rather than God's grace is rooted in a spiritual insecurity that does not understand the depths of God's complete acceptance of His children in Christ. Many believers have found that working to win the approval of God and man has only exhausted their strength. What we need is God's grace. It will be ours the moment we stop our frantic struggle and rest in His gracious and saving mercy.

God knew we could not keep His Law so He did something wonderful. God became a man—the person we know as Jesus Christ. In the form of a man, God lived the perfect requirements of the Law in our place. Romans 3:24 says, "Yet now God in his gracious kindness declares us not guilty. He has done this through Christ Jesus, who has freed us by taking away our sins." By receiving Christ as Savior and Lord, we can know that all our sins are forgiven and that someday we will be with Christ in heaven.

LAW AND GRACE INTERTWINED

But today the relationship between the Ten Commandments and God's grace has often been presented in a misleading way. Like two heavyweight fighters squaring off against one another in the ring, law and grace have been presented as two old warriors battling for our hearts and minds. But the fact is, law and grace are absolutely, beautifully intertwined. To seek to live in accordance with the Ten Commandments always results in blessings. Even non-Christians who choose to live in accordance with God's moral laws benefit from the positive results that follow, whereas even Christians who choose to violate those laws suffer the consequences.

Frequently I ask God if I am breaking any of His holy commands, and if so, to reveal what I can do to amend my ways. Why? My daily walk with Christ depends on it. The Ten Commandments are irrevocable, and we should know and obey each of them for our own well-being and for our pathway to grace. The Ten Commandments are positive influences in our lives. They help us build a productive and joyful life.

> *God's Laws do not bend or shift depending on the era in which we live, the circumstances in which we find ourselves, or the environment in which we were raised.*

Can you recite the Ten Commandments? This question is not meant to embarrass you, but to make a point. How can we live out God's commandments if we do not know them? And let's be honest. When most hear of the Ten Commandments, they do not think of God's unbendable moral code given to protect and provide an abundant life for them. They think of an angry God who is out to ruin their fun. But actually the opposite is true. God gave the Ten Commandments for our blessing.

When God gave the world the Ten Commandments, He gave us His transcendent standard. It goes beyond what we can see, hear, feel, or smell. It is a standard untouched by human hands. God's Laws do not bend or shift depending on the era in which we live, the circumstances in which we find ourselves, or the environment in which we were raised.

The Ten Commandments were given to the ancient Hebrews as a beacon to the world, a standard for everyone to know what God expects in relation to Him and others. For the believer, the Ten Commandments serve the larger purpose of showing us where we are in our spiritual growth. Our spiritual journey is so much more enjoyable when we know we are doing the things that are pleasing to God.

———————❖———————

"THOSE WHO OBEY MY COMMANDMENTS ARE THE ONES
WHO LOVE ME. AND BECAUSE THEY LOVE ME, MY FATHER
WILL LOVE THEM, AND I WILL LOVE THEM. AND I WILL
REVEAL MYSELF TO EACH ONE OF THEM."

—JESUS CHRIST

————————————————

2

God's Law Leads to Christ's Grace

Recently, I was seated next to a woman in an airplane. I asked if she was interested in reading through a small booklet, *The Four Spiritual Laws*, with me. After reading it, she explained that she was already a believer.

Because I pray every morning, in fact throughout the day, that God will lead me to the people whose hearts He has prepared for me to talk to about Him, I knew that God had something to say to her. So I gave her the booklet *Have You Made the Wonderful Discovery of the Spirit-Filled Life?* to read. This booklet presents many Scripture passages showing how to live a victorious Christian life in the power of the Holy Spirit. Out of the corner of my eye I saw that the woman read the booklet several times. Then I noticed tears streaming down her cheeks.

She turned to me and said, "Thank you so much for giving me this booklet. There is no way that you could know how appropriate it was. I am a Christian, but I am having an affair with a man who is waiting for me at the airport to take me to his home so we can live together. Now I know where I will turn to get the strength to withstand this temptation. I will turn down my friend and return to my husband."

What motivated this woman to return to her husband? It was the transforming power of God's Word, His Law, in her heart. The more she saw herself in the mirror of God's Word, the more she was driven to the need of God's grace to overcome her desire to leave her husband for another man. I never had to quote the seventh commandment to her, "Do not commit adultery." The Spirit of God made it clear to her.

> *We must never treat God's gracious forgiveness as a free ticket ... The expense of a life—God's only begotten Son—was paid upon a cruel Roman cross.*

How does this happen? God writes His Law upon our hearts the more we experience His loving grace and mercy.

THE TEN COMMANDMENTS IN YOUR LIFE

God gave the Ten Commandments to us for our blessing. There are three reasons why the Ten Commandments still hold an important place in the life of a believer and lead to a realization of grace.

THEY REFLECT THE NATURE OF GOD

The Bible never speaks of God as a mere abstract concept. Rather, it describes Him as a God who is very involved in His creation. And the Ten Commandments lie at the very heart of God's involvement with us. They reveal His will and His ways and His heart of grace, which are beneficial to us personally and to society at large. With the influence of the Ten Commandments working in our world, crime, adultery, and murder (to name just a few of society's ills) would be curbed. The fact is that every crime that takes place violates at least one of the Ten Commandments. Imagine all the pain and heartache that could be prevented if people used these commandments as their guide for living.

THEY PROMOTE RESPECT FOR GOD

Proverbs 1:7 says, "Fear of the LORD is the beginning of knowledge." A healthy, reverential fear of the God who created all heaven and earth, the eternal One who gave us life and who can take it, is the very bedrock of wisdom. Today, most Christians have lost that reverential fear of God and as a result have lost their basis for understanding. We clearly live at a time when believers, due to superficial knowledge of the holiness and majesty of our great God and Savior, treat Him in a far-too-casual manner.

In turn, our faith is not translating into moral reform in our personal lives or in our culture. I believe this ethical gap is caused by a "knowledge gap" with respect to God's character and laws. Furthermore, even those who have retained some intellectual understanding of God's Laws are increasingly losing a working knowledge of them. And when we lose our knowledge of God's Laws, we also lose our attitude of respect toward Him.

THEY REVEAL OUR GROWTH IN GOD

The Ten Commandments serve as a yardstick for our spiritual walk. God is the measure of all things. So how do we measure our lives before our God? By the Ten Commandments! Jesus said, "Those who obey my commandments are the ones who love me. And because they love me, my Father will love them, and I will love them. And I will reveal myself to each one of them" (John 14:21). According to Jesus, obedience to His commandments is a yardstick of the true spiritual condition of our lives. Although obedience to the Law does not produce the Spirit-filled life, we know we are living in the power of the Spirit to the degree we obey God's commandments and experience the power, joy, excitement, and adventure of the Christian life.

Today, we are a nation of people who claim to believe in God, and yet most of us know the Ten Commandments only secondhand. This has had a devastating effect. We are tempted to think of the Ten Commandments as little more than a set of quaint rules, completely outdated for our modern world. But as the well-known TV personality Ted Koppel once remarked in a speech at Duke University, "[The Ten Commandments] are not the Ten Suggestions."

BEWARE OF THE SEDUCTIVE EXTREMES

No one is capable of obeying God's Law in his or her own strength. But through the power of the Holy Spirit in us, we can lead productive, obedient lives. If we follow after the Holy Spirit and no longer obey the old, evil nature within us, we find the key to our liberation from a life of spiritual defeat. I cannot live the Christian life unless the Holy Spirit enables me, no matter how long I pray, fast, beg, and plead. I am not capable of pleasing God in my own strength and neither are you. The source of the Christian's strength lies only in God's grace and the Holy Spirit's empowerment.

Yet sometimes we devalue the grace we have in Christ. And at times our reliance on the Ten Commandments can contribute to our failings as believers. In our study on the Ten Commandments, we must avoid these two extremes: cheap grace and legalism. Both are unbiblical—and each one leads to particular problems in our Christian life.

THE CHARM OF CHEAP GRACE

"Cheap grace" is a term coined by the late German theologian Dietrich Bonhoeffer. His observations of the church still ring true in our day. "Cheap grace is the preaching of forgiveness without requiring repentance, baptism without church discipline, communion without confession, absolution without personal confession. Cheap grace is grace without discipleship, grace without the cross, grace without Jesus Christ, living and incarnate."[1] In essence, cheap grace is grace without complete surrender to the Lordship of Christ.

Obeying His commandments is not difficult if our hearts are full of thankfulness.

Clearly, the Bible teaches that salvation is free to all who would truly repent and trust in Christ. But it also teaches that those who receive salvation are responsible to live a life of good works—to "prove their repentance by their deeds" (Acts 26:20 NIV). Paul writes, "God saved you by his special favor when you believed. And you can't take credit for this; it is a gift from God. Salvation is not a reward for the good things we have done, so none of us can boast about it. For we are God's masterpiece. He has created us anew in Christ Jesus, so that we can do the good things he planned for us long ago" (Ephesians 2:8–10).

THE BEAUTY OF COSTLY GRACE

Jesus did not die for only those whom He called His friends. The Bible says that Jesus died for us even when we were God's enemies: "God showed his great love for us by sending Christ to die for us while we were still sinners" (Romans 5:8).

Bonhoeffer remarks about costly grace: "It is costly because it costs a man his life, and it is grace because it freely gives a man the only true life. It is costly because it condemns sin, and grace because it justifies the sinner ... Costly grace confronts us as a gracious call to follow Jesus, it comes as a word of forgiveness to the broken spirit and the contrite heart. Grace is costly because it compels a man to submit to the yoke of Christ and follow Him; it is grace because Jesus says: 'My yoke is easy and My burden light.'"[2] Costly grace calls us to follow Jesus Christ with our whole heart, mind, soul, and strength.

> *God will produce obedience to the Ten Commandments in us the way a tree bears its precious fruit.*

We must never treat God's gracious forgiveness as a free ticket to live as we want. The expense of a life—God's only begotten Son—was paid upon a cruel Roman cross so that we could receive His forgiveness and experience a life of peace and happiness. Costly grace inspires us to live by the Ten Commandments.

Costly Grace and the Exchanged Life. A great truth that helps overcome an attitude of cheap grace is what some call the "exchanged life." Paul writes to the church at Galatia, "I myself no longer live, but Christ lives in me. So I live my life in this earthly body by trusting in the Son of God, who loved me and gave himself for me. I am not one of those who treats the grace of God as meaningless. For if we could be saved by keeping the law, then there was no need for Christ to die" (Galatians 2:20–21).

Paul's new life was a testimony to the exchanged life. He did not treat the grace of God lightly. He allowed Christ to live His life in and through him. By grace, God offers to take away our sin in exchange for His righteousness. Paul writes, "God made Christ, who never sinned, to be the offering for our sin, so that we could be made right with God through Christ" (2 Corinthians 5:21). We exchange our depraved life of sin for Christ's life of righteousness.

Costly Grace and a Thankful Heart. When we look at the Ten Commandments, we see ten ways to practice costly grace and say "thank you" to Jesus. Obeying His commandments is not difficult if our hearts are full of thankfulness. Christ healed our broken relationship with our heavenly Father. God's judgment and wrath have been turned away. Eternal life is ours. And Christ's promise? To live inside us through His Holy Spirit—helping, comforting, and strengthening us each day in all of life's challenges. How can we respond with anything less than a life of total surrender and obedient gratitude?

THE LURE OF LEGALISM

On the opposite end of the spectrum from cheap grace is legalism. This is the belief that we can earn God's acceptance by observing religious rituals or by adhering to a set of religious works.

The writer of the book of Hebrews was very concerned about legalism. Jewish believers were reverting to meticulous adherence to the ceremonial law as a way of gaining God's acceptance. The writer contrasts a life of faith with trusting in works. Hebrews 6:7–8 says, "When the ground soaks up the rain that falls on it and bears a good crop for the farmer, it has the blessing of God. But if a field bears thistles and thorns, it is useless. The farmer will condemn that field and burn it."

No matter how much we may try to reform ourselves through legalistic behavior, we can never achieve the newness of life that God wants us to experience in Christ. Only Christ can change a human heart, give us spiritual life, and enable us to lead fruitful lives in accordance with God's Law.

THE BIBLE'S CURE FOR LEGALISM.

What is the answer to defeating legalism in our lives? Paul explains, "When we place our faith in Christ Jesus, it makes no difference to God whether we are circumcised or not circumcised. What is important is faith expressing itself in love" (Galatians 5:6).

> *"Those who obey My commandments are the ones who love me."*
> —Jesus Christ

The Christian life is not reams of rules that hang around our necks like a noose that tightens with every sin. It is a life of freedom. The Ten Commandments are designed to assist us in our exciting journey with Christ. If we try to produce the Spirit-filled life by obeying the Ten Commandments in our own effort, we are doomed to fail. But the Bible says to consistently walk by faith and to show love for God and others. Then God will produce obedience to the Ten Commandments in us the way a tree bears its precious fruit.

LIFE APPLICATION

Only as we rely on God's power can we truly attain the standard that God sets for our behavior. When we observe the Ten Commandments in the power of God's Spirit, they liberate us to do what is essential to please God. They tie us into the love of God by helping us get in step with what He has planned for our lives and His desire to protect us from wrongdoing and its consequences. His commandments unlock the blessings God has in store for us.

I highly encourage you to memorize the Ten Commandments. Regularly meditate on them and ask the Holy Spirit to help you obey them. They are keys that unlock God's love and blessings. The first group of commandments (1–4) addresses our obligations *toward God*, while the second group (5–10) speaks of our obligations *toward each other.* The first command follows the *shema* (Deuteronomy 6:4–9), which was a confessional statement central to Israel's life and worship. The second command comes from the laws of social order (Leviticus 19:18), which were a part of Israel's civil law.

As we study each one of the commandments, remember that obeying them is not to be a burden. Rather, it is a joyous experience with Christ when you follow these two simple principles: love God with your whole heart, soul, and mind; and love your neighbor as yourself.

---

1. Dietrich Bonhoeffer, *The Cost of Discipleship* (New York: Simon & Schuster, 1995), p. 44.

2. Ibid., p. 45

———————◆———————

"YOU SHALL HAVE NO OTHER GODS BEFORE ME."

EXODUS 20:3 NIV

———————————

3

Commandment #1
Keep God Above All Else

Many years ago in Brooklyn, New York, Thomas K. Beecher substituted as a speaker at the Plymouth Church for his famous brother, Henry Ward Beecher. Many curiosity seekers had come to hear the renowned Henry Beecher speak. When Thomas Beecher appeared in the pulpit instead, some people got up and started for the doors. Sensing that these people were disappointed because he was substituting for his brother, Thomas raised his hand for silence. Then he announced, "All those who came here this morning to worship Henry Ward Beecher may withdraw from the church. All who came to worship God may remain."[1]

Thomas Beecher was implying that all humans have the tendency to replace rightful focus on God with a preoccupation with other things. How many times have you been in a worship service and found yourself thinking about finances, a recent argument with your spouse, or the problems at your job? Our daily schedules also testify to the fact that we do not make God primary in our lives. Although we may not recognize or admit it, we let other things take God's place.

GOD EXPECTS YOUR WORSHIP

The first commandment spoke directly to the issue of whom ancient Israel was to worship. It says, "God instructed the people as follows: 'I am the LORD your God, who rescued you from slavery in Egypt. Do not worship any other gods besides me'" (Exodus 20:1–3). This law reflects the "great and foremost" commandment of the Old Testament: "You must love the LORD your God with all your heart, all your soul, and all your strength" (Deuteronomy 6:5). Jesus affirmed this commandment when He said, "You must love the Lord your God with all your heart, all your soul, and all your mind" (Matthew 22:37). Therefore, this commandment is also to be our top priority.

> *"If anyone wishes to come after Me, he must deny himself, and take up his cross, and follow Me." —Jesus Christ*

God gave this commandment to Moses at Mount Sinai not long after He had miraculously delivered His people out of Egypt. Without question, God was to be the number-one priority in the Hebrews' hearts and minds.

Why did God preface His first commandment with mention of His mighty deliverance of His people from Pharaoh's ruthless control? He wanted to jog the Israelites' memory of the plagues of Egypt and the parting of the Red Sea. Through those and other miracles, God reminded the ancient Hebrews, and reminds us today, that He alone has the power to set people free from spiritual bondage to sin. Therefore, He alone has the legitimate right to our worship. He will not tolerate any rival gods.

The world is a place of "false gods" that beg for our allegiance. Without exception, every false god, from Confucius to New Age paganism to materialism, says that people are basically good or that all man needs is a spiritual stimulant, not a Savior.

Do not waste your life chasing after earthly false gods that never satisfy. God's Word is filled with promises of tremendous blessings for the person who puts God first and rejects all man-made "gods." Come to the realization of the first commandment: *permanent* satisfaction is attainable only when you receive Christ by faith and give your *whole life* to the worship of God.

GOD HAS A RIGHT TO OUR WORSHIP

In addition to this first commandment, Scripture gives us several reasons why we should put God first in our lives.

First and foremost, God created us. The psalmist declares, "You made all the delicate, inner parts of my body and knit me together in my mother's womb" (Psalm 139:13). And Paul writes, "We are God's masterpiece. He has created us anew in Christ Jesus, so that we can do the good things he planned for us long ago" (Ephesians 2:10). Taken together, these verses teach that God is our Creator who designed us for a specific task—to live for Him in total devotion.

Second, God is our powerful Protector. The Bible says, "God is our refuge and strength, a very present help in trouble (Psalm 46:1 NASB).

No matter what threatening circumstances are encountered by those of us who truly trust our Lord, our all-powerful God is always with us. He constantly shields us from harm, even when we are unaware of the danger. Who is more worthy of our worship and devotion?

Third, God is the sovereign Ruler of the universe. One reason God refuses to share His honor is because only He is able to accomplish everything that He has planned for us. In His plan, He led the nation of Israel out of Egypt and through the wilderness to the Promised Land. Without Israel's *complete attention* focused on God, they would likely have gotten lost, or worse, perished along the way.

God likewise has a destination of incomparable blessing in store for all of His children—heaven. What part of your life are you allowing God to control on your way there? Are you inviting Him to direct your religious activities, but not the rest of your life?

> *When we put anything, good or bad, in place of God, we make that thing our god and we break this commandment.*

Many of us have been prone to wander about our own wastelands, distracted by cultural pressures. We become experts at compartmentalizing our lives, reserving God for a compartment on the Lord's Day, but on the next morning we set God aside and put on our business face or our homemaker face.

Jesus said, "If anyone wishes to come after Me, he must deny himself, and take up his cross, and follow Me" (Mark 8:34 NASB). If you are struggling in an area of your life, try putting God first in that area. For example, if you struggle with singleness, put God first by accepting whatever His plan is for your life. If you struggle with finances, put God first by giving Him back the fruits of your labor through your tithes and offerings, giving joyfully because of who He is and all He has done for you. Then He will lead you through all your difficulties.

WORSHIP GOD BY KEEPING HIM FIRST

G. Campbell Morgan, author and preacher at Westminster Chapel in London during the early twentieth century, observed, "Every man needs a god. There is no man who has not, somewhere in his heart, in his life, in the essentials of his being, a shrine in which is a deity whom he worships ... The question is whether the life and powers of man are devoted to the worship of the true God or to that of a false one."[2]

Please permit me to ask you a difficult question. What consumes your mind each day? Is it your work, your future, sex, money, or perhaps a loved one? The answer will help you determine what you have allowed to occupy God's rightful place of priority in your life.

One of my favorite, most meaningful promises from God's Word is recorded in Matthew 6:33, "Seek first his kingdom and his righteousness, and all these things will be given to you as well" (NIV).

Have you made seeking God and serving Him your highest priority? Consider how much effort, resources, and quality time you invest in personal interests, goals, or things versus what you commit to God. Whatever preoccupies your thoughts and your schedule is quite likely your "god."

WORSHIP GOD BY GIVING HIM THE GLORY

We tend to narrowly define worship as going to church on the Lord's Day. But worship is much, much more than that. The word "worship" comes from the old English *worth-ship*, which means "to ascribe worth or value to something or someone." It is recognizing and submitting to the awesome majesty of God in every area of life, moment by moment, seven days a week.

Worship not only involves singing and praising God, but

also includes how we think and live. A. W. Tozer eloquently writes, "Worship is to feel in your heart and express in some appropriate manner a humbling but delightful sense of admiring awe and astonished wonder and overpowering love in the presence of that most ancient Mystery, that Majesty which philosophers call the First Cause, but which we call Our Father Which Art in Heaven."[3]

Worship helps us begin to appreciate who God is and expresses an attitude of gratefulness and awe toward our holy Lord and Savior.

WORSHIP GOD THROUGH SACRIFICIAL LIVING

Because God is infinite and almighty, the first commandment distinguishes our worship of Him from all other earthbound devotion. Worship of God differs not only in *degree* from all other worship we may ascribe to people or things, but also in *kind*. God is not only *more important* than your job, family, and future, He is also *in charge* of your life.

Worship, then, must include our willingness to sacrifice anything God requires. God sacrificed His only Son at Calvary for you; now He may call upon you to sacrifice a personal goal, a relationship, or a job that does not represent His best for you. We must be willing to lay everything on our "worship altar" to God.

> Permanent *satisfaction is attainable only when you receive Christ by faith and give your* whole life *to the worship of God.*

WORSHIP GOD WITH WHOLEHEARTED LOVE

In Mark 12, Jesus is asked by a scribe, "Of all the commandments, which is the most important?"

Jesus replied, "The most important commandment is this: 'Hear, O Israel! The Lord our God is the one and only Lord. And you must love the Lord your God with all your heart, all your soul, all your mind, and all your strength'" (Mark 12:28–30). Jesus summarized the intent of the Law into a single concept—that we should love God with our *whole heart, soul, mind, and strength*. Here is a breakdown of what Jesus said:

> *Whatever preoccupies your thoughts and your schedule is quite likely your "god."*

- *Heart.* The devotion of my heart must be directed to God. The center of my being must be first aimed toward Him and His glory. He must be first in my ambitions and motives.
- *Soul.* My affections and emotions are to be ablaze with desire to worship and serve Him.
- *Mind.* My thought life must belong to Him so that my mind will be pure, disciplined, and ruled by His revealed will.
- *Strength.* All my energy, power, and strength must be surrendered to Him.

God desires and deserves nothing less than all our worship, praise, and thanksgiving.

LIFE APPLICATION

This first commandment is simple: God expects to be first in our lives. Therefore, anything that takes our focus and worship away from Him becomes like a god to us. It could even be a good thing, and often is a good thing: a relationship with another person, a job, the pursuit of success, education, or even sports. Sometimes it is something destructive, like an addiction to gambling, tobacco, alcohol, sex, or drugs. However, when we put anything, good or bad, in place of God, we make *that thing* our god and we break this commandment.

The world is a place of "false gods" that beg for our allegiance. They show up in the things we think are most important: money, family, friends, power, or possessions. What tops your list? Be honest.

If God isn't first in your life, here's one thing you can do to start putting Him first. Try getting up thirty minutes early tomorrow. Spend that time with God. Start by reading the first chapter in the gospel of John. Then talk to God about what you have read. Talk to Him about the day ahead. Make it a priority to spend time with God at the beginning of every day. Give God the first part of your day and He will be a part of your whole day! As you choose to put God first, He will change your life.

---

1. Michael P. Green, ed., *Illustrations for Biblical Preaching* (Grand Rapids, Mich.: Baker Books, 1990), illus. 506.

2. G. Campbell Morgan, *The Ten Commandments* (Chicago: The Bible Institute Colportage Association, 1901), pp. 18–19.

3. D. J. Fant, *A. W. Tozer* (Harrisburg, Penn.: Christian Publications, 1964), p. 90.

4

Commandment #2
Shun Idols

Possessions and property can destroy us. People whom we have placed on a pedestal can fall and shatter our trust. Goals and dreams can consume us. The world is a showcase of gods calling for our heart's commitment. Each one has the ability to shipwreck our futures on the rocks of despair.

But the true God has a better plan. He calls us to shun the gods of life and to worship Him alone. And God's promise for our obedience? To lavish upon us love and blessings in abundance.

WORSHIPING GOD'S WAY

The second of the Ten Commandments speaks to the issue of worshiping idols. It says, "Do not make idols of any kind, whether in the shape of birds or animals or fish. You must never worship or bow down to them, for I, the LORD your God, am a jealous God who will not share your affection with any other god! I do not leave unpunished the sins of those who hate me, but I punish the children for the sins of their parents to the third and fourth generations. But I lavish my love on those who love me and obey my commands, even for a thousand generations" (Exodus 20:4–6).

The first thing to notice about the second commandment is its relationship to the first commandment. At first glance, there does not appear to be a great distinction between the first two commandments. Both forbid false worship and both direct our hearts to God. However, there is an important difference. Whereas the first commandment tells us *Whom* to worship, the second tells us *how* to worship the one true God. Why does God tell us how we are to worship Him? Human nature is a peculiar thing. If left to our own devices, we are liable to do the right thing the wrong way.

> *Genuine worship of God does not come from religious activities, but is an* attitude.

Today our culture is marked by the sin of religious presumption. Many think God is impressed by formal religion but ignores the condition of their hearts. Because many have nice homes, fancy automobiles, and wonderful families, they think God favors them.

But underneath the superficial picture of that happy family is a gnawing awareness that all is not well. The things many dreamed about as children turn out to be little more than fleeting rainbows. These things satisfy for a while, but then as if dissolving into thin air, the thrill soon vanishes. Other people attend church and say prayers with their children before meals and at bedtime, hoping that their nominal faith will someday translate into joyful living. But sadly, for many that day never arrives.

There is an answer. Genuine worship of God does not

come from religious activities, but is an *attitude*. It does not come through nominal religion, but through an *exciting* personal *relationship*. It begins the moment you turn from the false gods of religion, avoid presumption, and set aside your pride to receive Christ as your Lord and Savior. Tell Him about your loneliness and despair—how the substitute gods have failed to provide you with lasting peace. Talk to God from your heart, and He will listen. He will bless you and your family if only you seek after Him with all your heart and soul.

No End to Idols

So far, we have considered the object of true worship— God—and have identified some of the substitute gods that may replace God's preeminence in our lives. We truly are a race that sets up false idols. When we consider the "how" of worship, we are thrust into a world of possible attitudes and actions that contend for our devotion. When Paul visited the ancient city of Athens, he discovered people worshiping so many idols that to make sure none had been overlooked, an altar was erected to the "unknown god"!

There are many ways we can practice idolatry without bowing before carved pieces of wood or stone. Permit me to point out several ways that we allow idolatry to pervade our attitudes.

The Idol of Greed

Paul considered greed such a pervasive sin that he put it in a group of other pernicious sins. He writes, "Therefore consider the members of your earthly body as dead to immorality, impurity, passion, evil desire, and greed, which amounts to idolatry" (Colossians 3:5 NASB). The excessive striving for more money, power, and things is idolatry. We become idolaters when we allow tangible things to become our gods and we therefore worship objects rather than our great God and Savior.

ANYTHING OR ANYONE GODLIKE

If we give power to anything other than God to save us, redeem us, or even lift us to a higher position in life, we make a graven image. The idol might be a doctor you hope will save you, a mate who will solve all your problems, or perhaps that house you believe will make you happy. Maybe your idol is a business or a political party. Anything we place our faith in besides God quickly becomes an idol.

We practice idolatry when we live by sight rather than by faith. Faith is believing in something we cannot see. But as humans, we have a tendency to desire the assurance of touch and sight so that we do not have to trust God in the spirit realm.

CULTURE'S DICTATES OVER GOD'S COMMANDMENTS

What is culture? It is ways of thinking, living, and behaving that define a people and underlie their achievements. It is a nation's collective mind, its sense of right and wrong, the way it perceives reality, and its definition of self. Culture is the morals and habits parents strive to instill in their children. It is the obligations we acknowledge toward our neighbors, our community, and our government. It is the worker's dedication to craftsmanship and the owner's acceptance of the responsibilities of stewardship. It is the standards we set and enforce for ourselves and for others, our definitions of duty, honor, and character. It is our collective conscience.

Culture becomes a personal idol when we supplant God's

Word with what society believes. Today, our culture's conscience is showing a greater, not lesser, tendency to place collective thinking above godly principles.

TAKE EVERY THOUGHT CAPTIVE

Paul is very clear on how to destroy both the personal and cultural idols that offend our heavenly Father. He writes, "We are destroying speculations and every lofty thing raised up against the knowledge of God, and we are taking every thought captive to the obedience of Christ" (2 Corinthians 10:5 NASB).

When your heart is focused on the needs of others, the idols that tempt you will flee.

Are you struggling in your thought life? Do you know someone else who suffers in the same way? The *inner struggle* is where the real battle against *all* idolatry lies. What are you doing to resist Satan's attacks? What are you doing to break his stronghold in the lives of others? Here are some suggestions on how to take *every* thought captive to Christ.

PRAY WITHOUT CEASING

We can pray every moment of the day. However, it is not the amount of time in prayer that matters to God so much as the quality and genuineness of one's prayer life. Additionally, I encourage you to keep your thoughts focused on the Lord and your heart singing with praises as you go about your daily tasks. Whenever you encounter an idol in your life, immediately turn away from it and reaffirm your obedience to God. Take a moment to worship Him as the supreme Creator God.

Also, pray against the cultural idols that pollute our land. Ask God to stem the immoral tide that has been unleashed. Be specific about the issues that affect your community and neighborhood. God will hear and respond.

LIVE ACCORDING TO GOD'S WORD, NOT FLEETING EMOTIONS

When Jesus was tempted by the Devil, He quoted Scripture. How much more must we rely on God's Word to keep us from the idolatry that tempts us? Be faithful in your devotional life and Bible study. Memorize Scripture

We practice idolatry when we live by sight rather than by faith.

verses and apply what you learn to your everyday life. The Word of God must be our constant guide.

SHARE YOUR FAITH WITH OTHERS

When your heart is focused on the needs of others, the idols that tempt you will flee. To the degree you "take captive" the personal idols of others through the ministry of the Word of God, the more your cultural idols are destroyed. These strongholds cannot stand up against the testimony of God's faithfulness. The more your friends and loved ones respond to God's love, the more they will also be able to recognize and put away the idols in their lives.

LIFE APPLICATION

There are many ways we can practice idolatry without actually bowing before carved pieces of wood or stone. Striving obsessively for more money, power, and things shuts God out of our lives. That's idolatry. Giving power to anything other than God to save us, redeem us, or even lift us to a higher position in life, replaces Him as the object of our worship. That's idolatry.

What in your life is more important to you than God? Are you willing to ask God to show you the idols in your life? Talk to Him in prayer about each one and ask Him to change your focus. Then, whenever you encounter an idol, immediately turn away from it and reaffirm your obedience to God. Choose today to give Him His rightful place in your heart. Worship Him alone and He will provide your needs and fill the empty places of your heart.

—————————— ❖ ——————————

"You shall not take the name of the Lord your God
in vain, for the Lord will not leave him unpunished
who takes His name in vain."

EXODUS 20:7 NASB

——————————————

5

Commandment #3
Revere the Lord's Name

After the American Civil War, the managers of the infamous Louisiana Lottery approached former Confederate General Robert E. Lee and asked if he would let them use his name in their scheme. They promised that if he did, he would become rich. Lee, a devout follower of Christ, straightened up, buttoned his gray coat, and shouted, "Gentlemen, I lost my home in the war. I lost my fortune in the war. I lost everything except my name. My name is not for sale, and if you fellows don't get out of here, I'll break this crutch over your heads!"

Misusing someone's name is always wrong. Have you ever asked an important friend if you could "drop his name" when attempting to secure a business deal? The only way that person will allow you to use his name is if he knows you and is confident that you will properly represent his name.

The third commandment speaks to this issue. It says, "Do not misuse the name of the LORD your God. The LORD will not let you go unpunished if you misuse his name" (Exodus 20:7). The term *Lord* (printed in capital letters in the English Old

Testament) is God's personal name and is the translation of the Hebrew word *Yahweh*. There is no name higher than God's name. His name is supreme among an entire universe of names. It is to be treated with a level of dignity and respect that reflects who God is.

WHAT'S IN A NAME?

In Jewish thought, a name is far more than an arbitrary identification. A name conveys the basic nature of the thing named. It represents the reputation of the one named and recalls the deeds the person has performed.

> *When we publicly profane God's name, we reduce Him in the world's eyes to a mere cultural icon.*

This concept shows how a name reflects the great worth and value of a person or object.

Throughout the Bible, God instructs parents to give a child a specific name that reflects who he is and foretells his mission in life. For example, Isaiah means "the salvation of the Lord." Ezekiel means "the strength of God." And Jesus means "savior" or "deliverer."

God also changes people's names as He enters their lives and assigns them a new direction or task. Part of God's covenant with Abram was to change his name to Abraham, which means a "father of many nations." Jesus changed Simon the fisherman's name to Peter, which means "rock." Saul of Tarsus was never the same after his encounter with the risen Lord on the road to Damascus. God gave him a new name, Paul, which mirrored his new heart for Christ. Paul means "small in stature, big in love."

Proper respect for the name of the Lord is so important

that Jesus instructed His followers to begin their prayers by showing utmost reverence for the name of God: "Our Father in heaven, hallowed be your name" (Matthew 6:9 NIV). To "hallow" means to consecrate, revere, or set apart. God's name is to be treated differently from all the other names on earth. Leviticus 22:32 declares, "Do not treat my holy name as common and ordinary."

God's name is so important that in heaven the very mention of it evokes worship. The name of the Lord was so sacred to the Orthodox Jews that they refused to utter it aloud. In their Scriptures, they replaced the name of God with a code word so they would not be tempted to say the name lightly.

Many people, however, take God's name lightly. We do this not only as a culture, but also in churches that have been influenced by contemporary society. The sacred name of God is used so casually that many people have no idea of the power behind it.

WHAT'S IN PROFANITY?

Most of us think of profanity when we hear the third commandment. How do you respond when someone uses profanity—especially when God's name is abused? God is our loving Father and we are His children. His Spirit lives within us, making our bodies His temple. He is awesome, mighty, powerful, and holy. God is offended when we use His name in a disrespectful way.

God's name will take on a whole new meaning as you cherish and esteem it.

Paul urges us not to engage in profanity or unclean speech.

He writes, "Don't use foul or abusive language. Let everything you say be good and helpful, so that your words will be an encouragement to those who hear them" (Ephesians 4:29).

Profanity is an affront to God's holiness for it calls into question who God is and what He has done.

When we speak God's name in a vile or cursing manner we profane both God's name and his reputation. Our God is holy, above all, without peer. He holds the stars in His hand and rules the universe. He is perfect in all His ways. Using His magnificent name in jest or as a curse is impugning His glory. As His children who have received eternal life because of His love for us, why would we ever want to cast a shadow on His name?

When we publicly profane God's name, we reduce Him in the world's eyes to a mere cultural icon. Such words have the effect of minimizing God's mighty power before others. Using God's name in a curse also denies what He has accomplished. People who use God's name in profanity deny what He has done for His people throughout history.

Paul encourages us to "let no unwholesome word proceed" from our mouths. He also says, "So put away all falsehood and 'tell your neighbor the truth' because we belong to each other" (Ephesians 4:25). God considers profane all words that question His goodness and holiness. We must never use God's name in a curse, throw God's name around for our own purposes, or speak about God in untrue terms, or we, too, will be guilty of profane lying.

MORE WALK THAN TALK

Although the third commandment addresses our speech, it has far more to do with our walk than our talk.

For many years, I have taught about the danger of living as

a carnal or worldly Christian. This is a believer whose life is not controlled by the Holy Spirit and who knows little about the abundant or fruitful life promised in the Scriptures. The presence of continuing sin in this person's life shows he does not understand his spiritual heritage in Christ. The word "vain" means "useless, void of any real value." The worldly Christian bears God's name as if it were meaningless, void of any real value or power.

> *God's name is so important that in heaven the very mention of it evokes worship.*

The answer for him is to discover the basic and revolutionary concept of how to be filled with the Holy Spirit. It is only then that one can live joyously and effectively for Christ.

DISHONORING GOD'S NAME IS COSTLY

The third commandment includes an incentive that should not go unnoticed. God says, "The LORD will not let you go unpunished if you misuse his name" (Exodus 20:7).

These are not the words of a mean, vindictive judge who gets pleasure in punishing people. Rather, God knows that we will suffer in life unless our hearts and minds place Him first in our thoughts and speech. So He disciplines us for our good. The Lord's discipline is *always* redemptive.

Dr. Billy Graham, commenting on God's discipline, said, "The Bible says, 'whom the Lord loveth He chasteneth.' If life were all easy, wouldn't we become flabby? When a ship's carpenter needed timber to make a mast for a sailing vessel, he did not cut it in the valley, but up on the mountainside where the trees had been buffeted by the winds. These trees, he knew, were the strongest of all. Hardship is not our choice; but if we face it bravely, it can toughen the fiber of our souls.

"God does not discipline us to subdue us, but to condition us for a life of usefulness and blessedness. In His wisdom, He knows that an uncontrolled life is an unhappy life, so He puts reins on our wayward souls that they may be directed into paths of righteousness."[1]

APPRECIATE THE VALUE OF HIS NAME

How can we resist using God's name in a profane way? Remember that taking God's name in vain reflects a *cavalier attitude* about God. The word "vain" means "useless, void of any real value." But is God without any real value? That is unthinkable.

> *"Whatever is in your heart determines what you say."*
> —*Jesus Christ*

Then ask yourself if taking His name in vain in such a casual fashion reflects the true nature and work of almighty God in your life.

Do not wait until your life is sinking in sorrow and distress to evaluate what is most precious to you. Appreciate the immense value of what God has done for you. Then God's name will take on a whole new meaning as you cherish and esteem it. Respect God's name. Revere it. Treasure it in your heart and in your speech, and God will bless you as you do.

LIFE APPLICATION

The third commandment speaks to the issue of honoring God's name. The term *Yahweh* is God's personal name and is generally translated "LORD." There is no higher name. God's name is supreme. It's to be treated with a level of dignity and respect that reflects who God is. Honor it, cherish it, and revere it. His name speaks volumes about His character—the awesome, majestic, and loving God whom we serve and worship. In His grace He permits us to bear His name before a watching world. Carry His name high; lovingly correct those who treat it disrespectfully. God will honor your faithfulness.

Sadly, though, God's name is used flippantly as everything from exclamations of excitement to swear words. Wherever and whenever people are talking—in office conversation, in movies, in TV shows, and even by interviewers and news anchors—God's name is misused.

Jesus says in Matthew 12:34, "Whatever is in your heart determines what you say." If we respect, love, and fear the Lord in our hearts, we won't dishonor His name with our lips. God's name speaks volumes about His character—the awesome, majestic, and loving God whom we serve and worship—and how we use His name says a lot about our love and respect for Him.

What do your words reveal about your relationship with your heavenly Father? Ask God to help you honor His name and commit yourself to using God's name only in a reverent way.

---

1. "The Chastening Love of God," *The Pastor's Story File* (Platteville, Colo.: Saratoga Press), May 1991.

---◆---

"REMEMBER THE SABBATH DAY, TO KEEP IT HOLY."

EXODUS 20:8 NASB

6

Commandment #4
Respect the Lord's Day

Wandering deep into the dark forest, Tom and Betty looked for the perfect tree. "A large oak would work best," said Tom.

"I'll see if I can find one," replied Betty.

The year was 1941, shortly after the start of World War II. The newlywed couple had been married for two weeks and planned to settle down in the same town they both grew up in. Then Tom was called to serve his country.

"Here's an oak!" exclaimed Betty. It was an old oak with massive limbs.

Tom and Betty looked at each other, agreeing that this was indeed the right tree. Tom drew his knife and began to carve their initials in the tree's trunk. "It will be here forever, my love," said Tom.

"Someday soon, you'll be back," Betty said, a tear sliding down her cheek. "But until then this tree will stand as a reminder of what we have."

Like Tom and Betty's initials carved on that tree, God carved the Sabbath day observance into our week. It stands as a reminder of God's incredible love for His creation. Understanding our fleshly limitations, He gave us a day to rest in Him from all our hectic labors. The Sabbath also reminds us of God's great love in Christ, in whom we can find rest for our weary souls.

REST FOR THE GLORY OF GOD

The fourth commandment says, "Remember to observe the Sabbath day by keeping it holy. Six days a week are set apart for your daily duties and regular work, but the seventh day is a day of rest dedicated to the LORD your God. On that day no one in your household may do any kind of work. This includes you, your sons and daughters, your male and female servants, your livestock, and any foreigners living among you. For in six days the LORD made the heavens, the earth, the sea, and everything in them; then he rested on the seventh day. That is why the LORD blessed the Sabbath day and set it apart as holy" (Exodus 20:8–11).

Keeping one day in seven holy to the Lord is required by the fourth commandment. Although it was created for our benefit, the type of rest required on the Sabbath day is a special *rest to the Lord*. It is a rest that is to be observed on the Lord's terms and for *His glory*.

Working constantly may be visible proof that deep inside we do not trust God.

In the New Testament, the "Lord's Day," Sunday, replaced the Jewish Sabbath for many followers of Christ because the Lord Jesus rose from the dead on Sunday (John 20:1). The Day of Pentecost also occurred on Sunday (Acts 2:1). As a result, the first Christians came together on Sunday, the first day of the week, to worship and celebrate communion (Acts 20:7).

A Cultural Tug-of-War

Once there was a day when Sunday observance and rest was a mainstay of our culture. That has changed. Today, retail stores and professional sports operate seven days a week. What is the root of the problem?

As a society, we value productivity above everything else. We are restless. We cannot sit still long enough to rest and reflect. We have to be doing something productive even when we are resting. We frantically jog, rush to see a movie, or trim those hedges before another weekend slips by. Most in our culture today would scoff at the idea of taking a day off to do nothing but honor the Creator and rest in His care. However, there are several reasons why this law still needs to be observed today.

All Creation Requires Rest

God commanded that no one was to work on this sacred day, including livestock. This is because ancient tribes were mainly subsistence farmers, making just enough to feed their families. To them, resting an entire day was not an option. God had to intervene or people would have worked themselves and their animals into an early grave!

The Sabbath rest was also for the protection of the land. Any good farmer knows the principle of crop rotation. If a farmer continues to grow the same crop in the same field year after year, he will permanently damage the soil. But if you allow the soil to rest some years, the nutrients and the moisture in the soil replenish and the field will continue to yield healthy crops. Today, the federal government pays some farmers to set aside certain fields so they will avoid burning out the soil.

A DAY TO WORSHIP GOD

How can we keep the Lord's Day holy if we sleep in late, watch football games, or do any other activity instead of worshiping God? Although I don't see anything wrong with watching decent television programs or reading the newspaper on the Lord's Day, my major attention all day is on God.

Worshiping God on the Lord's Day by attending a Bible-preaching church is part of our responsibility in putting God first in our lives. Not only do church services help us focus on God, they also help us encourage each other to serve Him. Hebrews 10:25 commands believers, "Let us not neglect our meeting together, as some people do, but encourage and warn each other, especially now that the day of his coming back again is drawing near." When we set aside the first day of the week to worship God, we are showing that He has the priority. It helps us develop a healthy awe of God all through the week.

JUST TO REFLECT ON ALL THAT GOD HAS DONE

The Bible says that God rested after working. "On the seventh day, having finished his task, God rested from all his work" (Genesis 2:2). What does the Bible mean when it says that God rested? Was He tired? Had He strained a muscle? Does the Bible assume that God needed a rest after six days of hard work like anyone else? Of course not.

God rested in another sense. His rest was more a time of

reflection about His marvelous creation. Genesis 1:31 says, "God saw all that He had made, and behold, it was very good" (NASB).

When we rest from all our labor, we are afforded an opportunity to reflect on God's goodness to us. Whether we rest in the beauty of His creation or in the way God brings peace and blessing to our lives through Christ, we are surrounded by testimonies to God's matchless goodness. Surely we can take one day to sit back and bask in all that God has done for us.

A Sign of Our Trust in God

There is nothing wrong with hard work. We must use the resources and talents God gave us to earn a living, care for our homes, and provide for the needs of our children. But to work

> *[God's] rest was more a time of reflection about His marvelous creation.*

constantly without adequate reflection and worship is a fundamental trust issue. If you truly trust God to provide for you, then you will do as He requires and take time to honor Him one day a week, on the Lord's Day.

Working constantly may be visible proof that deep inside we do not trust God. You say you trust God, but do you really? Often our actions speak louder than our words. The intoxication with long hours of work on the Lord's Day says: "I trust God, but just in case He doesn't pull through, I need an ace in the hole!"

First Timothy 6:17 records, "Their trust should be in the living God, who richly gives us all we need for our enjoyment." God promises not only to give us our needs, but He even cares about our enjoyment! Time and time again the Bible recounts how God wants us to trust Him for all our needs.

Have you ever heard a person say, "I need thirty-two hours in a day to get everything done?" God gives us only twenty-four hours in a day to accomplish all He has given us to do. But did you know that *prayer* is one way we can actually *become more productive*?

When you pray you are actually saving time! Prayer is a way to release the miracle-working power of God in your life. Through prayer, God can increase your productivity, eliminate obstacles that slow down your work, and provide resources that will quickly facilitate your objectives. In the end, you will actually find yourself ahead!

Imagine the time you could save each week by praying on the Lord's Day rather than working! Are you behind on a special project or on your bills? It is only natural to think you need to work on the Lord's Day in order to "catch up." But God says to pray. If you rest on that day, trust God with your needs, and pray, then God will provide for you and your family in a marvelous way.

A BLESSING, NOT A CURSE

Yes, all the commandments have as their ultimate aim the glory of God. But as I have said repeatedly, the Ten Commandments also exist to bless you and your family. Look at this story from the book of Mark:

One Sabbath day as Jesus was walking through some grainfields, His disciples began breaking off heads of wheat. The Pharisees who saw them said to Jesus, "They shouldn't be doing that! It's against the law to work by harvesting grain on the Sabbath."

Jesus replied, "Haven't you ever read in the Scriptures what King David did when he and his companions were hungry? He went into the house of God (during the days when Abiathar was high priest), ate the special bread reserved for the priests alone, and then gave some to his companions. That was breaking the law, too."

Then Jesus said to them, "The Sabbath was made to benefit people, and not people to benefit the Sabbath. And I, the Son of Man, am master even of the Sabbath!" (Mark 2:24–28).

The Pharisees completely missed the spirit of the fourth commandment. Jesus said that the Sabbath was instituted to benefit people, not to make people slaves to the Sabbath. It was supposed to be a blessing, not a curse. A time for rest, worship, and reflection, not for watching your every little step. Because the Sabbath was made for man, we must never treat it *legalistically*.

> *Living and resting in Christ alone for salvation is the true spiritual meaning of the Sabbath.*

THE LORD'S DAY POINTS TO THE BLESSING OF ETERNAL LIFE IN CHRIST

Like all the commandments and rituals of the Old Testament, this commandment points to our risen Lord. Living and resting in Christ alone for salvation is the true spiritual meaning of the Sabbath.

The writer of Hebrews says, "So there is a special rest still waiting for the people of God. For all who enter into God's rest will find rest from their labors, just as God rested after creating the world. Let us do our best to enter that place of rest. For anyone who disobeys God, as the people of Israel did, will fall … That is why we have a great High Priest who has gone to heaven, Jesus the Son of God. Let us cling to him and never stop trusting him" (Hebrews 4:9–11, 14).

> *God carved the Sabbath day observance into our week.*

In Christ alone we discover perpetual rest from sin and worry. On the first Sabbath, God rested forever, having completed His marvelous work of creation. Likewise, Christ said at the cross, "It is finished." His work of redemption on behalf of the world was completed at Calvary.

What does God require from us in response to Christ's finished work? It is to receive Christ into our hearts by faith. Once we have, God promises to freely pardon all our sins, never to forsake us. The believer has eternal assurance that his sin is forever forgiven and cast as far as the east is from the west. God will remember it no more.

We honor God when we obey the fourth commandment. And we build up our bodies and minds as we fulfill the pattern of work and rest created by God. We must keep our perspective on God's commandment to take time out to worship Him.

LIFE APPLICATION

God himself models this commandment for us. He created the world in six days and rested on the seventh. He declared the seventh day blessed and holy. For us, it's a day to rest, worship God, and reflect on all He's done and on His goodness. Taking a day off from our work to focus on

Him demonstrates our trust in Him. Whether we rest in the beauty of His creation or in the way God brings peace and blessing to our lives through Christ, we are surrounded by testimonies to God's matchless goodness.

Today, thank God for the privilege of setting aside one special day a week to honor and worship Him. Ask the Holy Spirit to help you use the Lord's Day as a day to focus on God and to help you be more productive during the rest of the week. Then, by faith and in obedience, adjust your schedule to honor the Lord with your Sabbath.

———————❖———————

"HONOR YOUR FATHER AND YOUR MOTHER,
THAT YOUR DAYS MAY BE PROLONGED IN THE LAND
WHICH THE LORD YOUR GOD GIVES YOU."

EXODUS 20:12 NASB

————————————

7

Commandment #5
Honor Your Parents

O nce there was a man, his wife, and their four-year-old son who lived in a fine house. In time, the man's father became old and needed care, so they brought him into the home to live. But there was a problem. The old father's hands trembled when he ate, and many times he missed his mouth and dribbled his food onto the tablecloth.

Putting up with her father-in-law aggravated the wife. She said, "I can't have this. It interferes with a woman's right to happiness." So the couple set the old man on a stool in the corner of the kitchen where they gave him his food in an earthenware bowl. From then on, he ate in the corner, staring at the family with his vacant old eyes.

Soon his hands trembled so much that he dropped the bowl and it broke. His daughter-in-law was incensed. "If you are a pig," she said, "you must eat out of a trough." So the couple made him a small wooden trough and put all his food in it.

One day at mealtime, the couple noticed their young son

playing with some bits of wood. "What are you doing?" the father asked.

With a big smile, he said, "I'm making a trough to feed you and Momma out of when I get big."

The fifth commandment reads, "Honor your father and mother. Then you will live a long, full life in the land the LORD your God will give you" (Exodus 20:12). This law is the first to instruct us how to act toward *each other*. The very first law

> *Obedience always leads to spiritual blessings and a long, full life.*

concerning our earthly relationships speaks about how to treat our parents, because the way we learn to treat them affects how we behave toward all authority throughout our life. Since God has commanded that we honor our parents, we can know that it pleases Him when we do so. It also benefits our own well-being when we honor them, because we are being obedient. Obedience leads to spiritual blessings and a long, full life.

WHY HONOR PARENTS?

When I was growing up, it never occurred to me to dishonor my parents. But I was raised in a very different culture. Most young people learned, through proper discipline, to be respectful to their parents and elders. They were taught to avoid anything that would dishonor their family.

But in today's dysfunctional families, conflicts reign. Many young people seldom eat a meal with the rest of the family. Family members are busy with so many distractions that family life suffers. Some children live with parents who are alcoholics, drug addicts, or abusive. There is no love, no unity, no harmony. It is hard for these young people to imagine loving their father and mother.

But respecting our parents is not optional—no matter what the circumstances are. There are several reasons why God commands us to honor our parents.

It Pleases God

The root meaning of *honor* is "to be heavy or weighty." Thus, we are to treat each parent as a "weighty" person in society, as someone who is important and worthy of respect. So important was parental respect in the Old Testament that a rebellious son was to be stoned to death to protect society (Deuteronomy 21:20–21).

The New Testament often speaks of lack of parental respect, but no passage is as direct as this one in Romans: "Their lives became full of every kind of wickedness, sin, greed, hate, envy, murder, fighting, deception, malicious behavior, and gossip. They are backstabbers, haters of God, insolent, proud, and boastful. They are forever inventing new ways of sinning and are disobedient to their parents" (Romans 1:29–30). Doesn't this describe what is happening today?

On the other hand, the Bible celebrates children who honor their parents. Proverbs 10:1 says, "A wise child brings joy to a father." Proverbs 15:5 tells us, "Only a fool despises a parent's discipline; whoever learns from correction is wise."

We have no justifiable reason in God's eyes to ever treat our parents with disrespect. That is the responsibility God has given us as sons and daughters. We please Him when we obey the fifth commandment.

IT MAINTAINS GOD'S ORDER

Why does the Bible place such emphasis on honoring parents? Because as goes the family, so goes society. The first and most prominent authority figures in our lives are our parents. If we do not learn to respect, honor, and obey them, we will not learn to honor and esteem any earthly authority. And a society without respect for authority will soon crumble.

IT BENEFITS OUR OWN WELL-BEING

The world is filled with children who desperately long for reconciliation with their parents and with God. If you are not demonstrating proper respect to your parents, you will no doubt want to take appropriate steps to reconcile with them and begin anew.

A young woman who was on our staff had experienced conflict with her father through the years until finally it turned into physical abuse. At seventeen, she left home in anger, saying, "I never want to see you again. Don't ever contact me. As far as I am concerned, you are dead."

She didn't talk to her father for five years. During this time, she was homeless, so she became a prostitute and a drug addict. Then one day she met a Campus Crusade for Christ staff member who led her to Christ. Soon after, she attended a Christmas conference in Chicago where I was speaking. Present were about two thousand student conferees.

One evening, I spoke on the importance of loving and honoring your parents. When I concluded I said, "Go to your room, get on the phone, and call your parents and tell them that you love them. Or write them a note and say, 'I love you and am grateful for all you have done for me.' Even if they are alcoholics or drug addicts, you are commanded to honor your father and mother. Jesus said to love your enemies, so even if your parents have acted like enemies to you, you must love them."

The next morning, this beautiful young girl came to see me along with a staff member. She told the story of her severed relationship with her father and how he had affected her life. She described how she had ended up on the streets homeless, a prostitute, and a drug addict—and how she had tried to kill herself several times.

She said, "As you were speaking last night, the Holy Spirit prompted me to call my parents and tell them that I love them. I could hardly wait to get out of the meeting. As soon as I got back to my room, I called my parents.

As goes the family, so goes society.

I told them that I love them and that I am so sorry for all I said and did to them. I explained how I received Christ as my Savior and how my life has changed. They treated me so warmly, and they were so happy that I called. Now I can hardly wait to see them."

She personally experienced the powerful blessing of honoring her parents. An incredible weight had been lifted from her life, and Christ had set her free.

IT LEADS TO GOD'S PROMISE OF A LONG, FULL LIFE

The fifth commandment carries a promise that says, "Then you will live a long, full life in the land the LORD your God will give you" (Exodus 20:12). At the time the fifth commandment was given, the Jews had been freed from Egypt and were traveling toward the Promised Land. God wanted them to know that national stability and longevity would result if they honored their parents as a culture. The blessing is also promised to us as believers.

Building anything that results in stability and longevity takes effort and persistence. For example, scattered along five hundred miles of California's northern coastline lie hidden valleys filled with some of nature's most majestic skyscrapers—the redwoods.

As regal as they appear, these incredible giants of the wilderness sprang from seeds so tiny that twelve can fit on a penny with room left over; more than a million squeezed together would weigh only a pound. Yet each is capable of producing a tree weighing tons.

The right combination of soil, moisture, and sunlight is required for the redwood's proper growth. The soil is crucial.

In the redwood, we see a picture of the blessings of longevity and strength that a nation can enjoy when it affords the family a place of prominence. When children are nurtured in the right environment of loving parents and give parents due respect, our nation will grow and prosper. Respect for parents and authority will stimulate the right kinds of relationships that help society to function as it should for the well-being of its citizens. Disrespect for parents and authority, however, will destroy the climate that makes a culture flourish.

LOVE WITHOUT HYPOCRISY

Honoring our parents from our hearts means that our honor must go beyond mere words. Unless we back up our words with actions, we become hypocritical. Jesus chided the Pharisees of His day for honoring God with their lips but not in their deeds. He said, "You hypocrites! Isaiah was prophesying about you when he said, 'These people honor me with their lips, but their hearts are far away'" (Mark 7:6–7).

Abandonment is one of the biggest fears of the elderly. We need to assure our parents that we will be there for them until the end of their lives. And if nursing home care becomes necessary, elderly parents still need love, care, and regular visits. Our parents cared for us for many years before we could care for ourselves. Care in their older years is an expression of gratitude, as well as an act of obedience.

Respect for parents and authority will stimulate the right kinds of relationships that help society to function.

The word *honor* carries the idea of prizing something highly, of taking care of someone, showing affection, and making sure that no evil befalls him. God does this for us. The psalmist declares, "He will call upon Me, and I will answer him; I will be with him in trouble; I will rescue him and honor him" (Psalm 91:15 NASB). We must do the same for our parents.

In spite of all their flaws and faults, most parents have tried, to the best of their abilities, to raise their children right. All that most parents want in return is love and respect. We honor them when we love them, give them emotional and financial support, and talk to them. Loving actions are as necessary as words.

Have you ever heard someone say, "I wish I had just one more chance to tell my parents I love them"? Do not allow yourself to get caught in this situation. Tell them today and every time you are together. And by all means, show them. As the old saying goes, "When all is said and done, more is said than done."

LIFE APPLICATION

God desires that we treat each parent as someone who is worthy of respect and honor, even if—perhaps especially if—our parents haven't acted in ways that we deem worthy of honor. We cannot control the way that others act; however, the important issue is how we act or react to others' actions. God did not say honor your parents if … He said honor them, period, plain and simple!

For some, honoring parents is easy because their parents have been loving and fair. Others have difficulty because their parents have not fulfilled their roles in a godly way. But all of us can honor our parents regardless of our circumstances.

We start by forgiving them. This can be a very difficult step, particularly if you have been deeply hurt by one or both of your parents. However, we have all been hurt and disappointed by our parents at some time. With God's help, we can forgive any hurtful experience. Sometimes this is a long process. Ask the Holy Spirit to fill you with God's forgiveness. The result will always be healing—at least in the heart of the forgiver.

> *Loving actions are as necessary as words.*

The fifth commandment can yield incredible blessings to anyone who obeys it. The world is full of earthly relationships—the most important of which is between family members. Yet our family relationships are often the most difficult to nurture. We must continue to make every effort to draw our strength from God's Holy Spirit to make the relationship we have with our parents pleasing to Him. You should honor your parents by respecting their God-given position even if they have done nothing to deserve your honor. The best way is to tell your parents today and every time you are together that you love them. Take the time to show them that you love them. That's God's clear commandment to all of us.

The by-products of honoring and loving our parents can be numerous. The way we treat our spouses and children will change for the better immediately, our relations with others should greatly improve, and our relations with those in authority over us will radically improve. Choosing to obey God always reaps positive benefits.

8

Commandment #6
Value Human Life

Mrs. Gena Foster, a thirty-four-year-old mother of three, entered a freeway in Birmingham, Alabama, on her way to pick up her youngest child from school. As she merged into traffic, she accidentally cut in front of Mrs. Shirley Henson, a company secretary who was hurrying home to walk her two Labradors. Shirley, disturbed by the merging vehicle, flashed her lights.

Then things began to escalate. Gena put on her brakes, and an altercation between the two vehicles began that lasted for several miles. Soon, both women pulled off on a side road and stopped at a traffic light.

Gena got out of her sports car and approached the door of Shirley's car. According to police reports, Shirley, a former Cub Scout leader with a teenage son, reached over to her glove box, took out the gun she kept there, lowered her window, and shot Gena in the face. Gena died at the side of the road. The life of a mother of three was gone in an instant.

Gena Foster's death is an example of what can happen because of the evil that lurks in all our hearts. The deaths that too often accompany road rage and other violent incidents prove that deep in each person's heart lies the potential to do great harm to another human being. Murder is not a crime reserved for the dregs of society. Given the right set of circumstances, anyone is capable of it. Shirley Henson was an average middle-class suburbanite. Nevertheless, in a flash, she was responsible for a murder and a precious life was lost.[1]

ONLY THE CREATOR DECIDES

The sixth commandment says, "Do not murder" (Exodus 20:13). Why did God give us this commandment? Only the Creator of all life may say when one should end. God values every human life. Humans are the pinnacle of His creation.

Man's attempts to supplant God in matters that pertain to human life always result in disaster. For example, left unchallenged, godless trends in science result in evil having full control over life issues. Eugenics and fetal tissue research, for example, are but natural outgrowths of the world's current devaluation of human life and its deification of science.

God values every human life. Humans are the pinnacle of His creation.

To understand these moral issues, we must make a distinction between "killing" and "murder." Not all killing is murder. The narrow scope of the sixth commandment focuses on the taking of an "innocent" human life by another human, often with premeditation. According to the great biblical scholar Charles Ryrie, the word translated "kill" in this sixth commandment is used 49 times in the Old Testament. In each case, the word in the original Hebrew language means "to murder with premeditation."

Furthermore, each time the sixth commandment is repeated in the New Testament, a word is always used that means "to murder" in the sense of taking innocent life.

At first glance, this command looks extremely clear. But there are many contemporary questions related to the taking of a life. It takes prayer, thorough study of the Scriptures, and careful discernment to apply this commandment to some of the issues facing us.

To begin to understand God's perspective on murder, let's ask, "What is it not?"

CAPITAL PUNISHMENT IS NOT MURDER

According to Genesis 9:5–6, capital punishment is the penalty for murder. God said to Noah and his family, "Murder is forbidden. Animals that kill people must die, and any person who murders must be killed. Yes, you must execute anyone who murders another person, for to kill a person is to kill a living being made in God's image."

Why the death penalty for murder? First of all, because God created human life, it's His call as to when it can be morally ended. But more fundamentally, it's because man was created in the very image of God; therefore, taking the life of a person is to attack the Creator God. Imagine that someone destroyed something you made and cherished. Would you not feel as though you had been personally attacked? This simple analogy, however, does not approach the seriousness of murder. God values every human's life, and humans are the pinnacle of His creation. There is no clearer way to assault the Creator than to murder a living person—His finest creation.

Many people argue that capital punishment is state-sanctioned murder and is therefore against the sixth commandment. However, these people are mistaken. Capital punishment is not about harming the innocent, but is executing justice upon the guilty who have taken a human life with forethought. Therefore, this form of killing is acceptable in God's eyes.

MILITARY DEFENSE OF A NATION IS NOT MURDER

Sergeant Alvin C. York was the most celebrated soldier of World War I. To this day, his story remains a testimony of one man's heroic faith and bravery. But those who knew York as a young man would never have guessed he would become the most decorated soldier of his time.

Born in rural Tennessee in 1887, York was the third of eleven children. His deadly accurate shooting ability became evident early in his life. But York was also a troubled young man. He spent much of his early years drinking liquor and gambling. Then, following the death of a close friend in a bar fight, he gave his life to Christ.

By the time he was drafted for military service, one of the best marksmen in the South did not believe he could kill another man, even in war. York came from a long line of men who had fought for their country since the American Revolution, yet he had difficulty reconciling his patriotic duty with his faith. "I wanted to be a good Christian and a good American too," he said. "My religion and my experience told me not to go to war, and the memory of my ancestors ... told me to get my gun and go fight. I didn't know what to do ... There was a war going on inside me, and I didn't know which side to lean to."

York was soon sent overseas. After seeking the counsel of some of his superiors and praying to God, York was eventually convinced that there is such a thing as a "moral war." And indeed, God had directly commanded His own people on several occasions to destroy enemies in various wars. Clearly there had to be a distinction between God's sixth command, which He gave to His people at Mount Sinai, and his direct commands a short while later demanding that those same Israelites utterly destroy their Canaanite enemies. God differentiates between a human life taken in war and a human life taken in murder.

> *There is no clearer way to assault the Creator than to murder a living person— His finest creation.*

The dramatic events of October 8, 1918, at the battle of Argonne, etched the name of Alvin York in history. York's patrol was ordered to take out German machine-gun fire. With only a rifle and a pistol, York helped kill more than twenty Germans. His actions led to the surrender of 132 enemy soldiers.

York would never see great wealth from his daring feat. Rather, the southern gentleman went back to his Tennessee home and spent what little money he earned from lecturing to enhance educational standards for the youth of Fentress County, Tennessee, and to start a small Bible school.[2]

SELF-DEFENSE IS NOT MURDER

Although warfare is often a form of self-defense, the two are not identical. Warfare is a collective act of the citizens of a nation, whereas self-defense is an individual act not related to military action.

Self-defense is not so much something that people need to learn as it is an instinctive part of nature. In fact, all animals and even some plants defend themselves when threatened. Thus, God never needed to teach His people that it is permissible to defend themselves. But He did lay down laws for the nation of Israel that limited the use of self-defense. (See Exodus 21:12–22:3.)

THE SANCTITY OF LIFE

We have seen that the Bible does not consider all killing to be morally wrong. Yet the Bible is clear that we are to consider all human life sacred. From the most vulnerable to the most hardy, God considers every person precious.

Yet our culture devalues the sanctity of human life. We have called murder by other names and made it seem acceptable. Taking into account all that the Bible has to say about it, we should always stand for the sanctity of human life and defend those who are helpless to defend themselves. That includes the unborn, adults with handicaps or incurable diseases, the elderly, and the world's oppressed. As believers in the God of life, we must always affirm human life and even defend it. Let's look at several social issues that God calls murder.

The Bible is clear that we are to consider all human life as sacred.

ABORTION IS MURDER

Many people do not realize that abortion is murder. Abortion is murder because it takes the life of an innocent human—in this case, the most innocent and defenseless in our society. Every human's life begins from the very moment of conception. Psalm 139:13–14 (NIV) tells us, "For you created my inmost being; you knit me together in my mother's womb. I praise you because I am fearfully and wonderfully made; your works are wonderful." The fetus is not just a blob of flesh; it is a human being created in the image of God. When we take the life of that child, we violate the sixth commandment.

Since *Roe v. Wade*, the infamous American landmark Supreme Court decision in 1973, approximately 40 million babies have been aborted—an average of 4,000 each day! The overwhelming majority of all abortions, 95 percent, have been done as a means of birth control. Of the remaining 5 percent, only 1 percent were performed because of rape or incest, 1 percent because of fetal abnormalities, and 3 percent due to the mother's health problems.

If someone you know is considering an abortion, take a stand for the sanctity of human life. Adoption is the courageous alternative for an unplanned pregnancy. That child is so precious. Contact your local pro-life group for help in doing what's right.

EUTHANASIA IS MURDER

Euthanasia is murder because it takes life rather than supports those who need physical, emotional, or financial help. It advocates abandonment rather than compassion. The following excerpt from *The New York Times* is chilling:

> The American Department of Justice, in a detailed memorandum explaining the government's aims regarding its code, has announced its intention to authorize physicians to end the sufferings of incurable patients. The memorandum, still lacking the force of law, proposed that "it shall be made possible for physicians to end the intractable

pain of incurable patients, upon request, in the interests of true humanity."[2]

The church must pray that this trend goes no further in public policy and that current law in support of euthanasia is soon reversed. The church must also take the lead in ministering to those who suffer so much pain that they despair of life.

GENOCIDE IS MURDER

Genocide is in total opposition to God's values, vested in the lives of a group of people whom He created. It is murder on a grand scale. Genocide is crime on a different scale from all other types of murder. It is an effort to completely exterminate a national, ethnic, racial, or religious group. Genocide is therefore a "crime against humanity."

Genocide is proof that, without God, man is absolutely inhumane. Rather than civilization advancing morally, we are plummeting into a moral abyss. Our sinfulness shows that we cannot survive without God's standards, the Ten Commandments, and the life-giving power of the Holy Spirit.

SUICIDE IS MURDER

Abortion, euthanasia, and genocide are premeditated forms of murder that stem from a diminished view of the sanctity of life. Nevertheless, another premeditated form of killing also results from a low valuation of life. It is suicide. Those who contemplate this action are placing a low value on something that God values very highly—their own life.

Clearly suicide represents Satan's lie that all hope is lost. But the Bible says that Satan is a liar. He has come to "steal and kill and destroy" (John 10:10). But Jesus came to give abundant life! If the thought of harming yourself enters your mind, please pray, quote Scripture, and listen to praise and worship music. And then seek the confidence of a mature member of Christ's body—a Christian of righteous counsel—who can edify and support you. Also, do not hesitate to seek medical and professional attention, preferably from a Christian physician or counselor. By talking to God in prayer, listening to Him through His Word, interacting personally and authentically with His body, and enlisting professional care, your mind can be filled with hope. As you meditate on God and His Word, the evil schemes will be defeated.

LIFE APPLICATION

The Bible is clear that we're to consider *all human life* sacred. God considers every person precious. That includes the unborn, individuals with handicaps or incurable diseases, the elderly, and the world's oppressed. As believers in the God of life, we must always affirm life and defend it.

Do you find yourself thinking: "Well, at least this is one of the commandments that I'm not

> *Without God, man is absolutely inhumane.*

guilty of breaking. I've never taken someone else's life." Jesus always took the law to the next level. He knew that many of His followers obeyed the letter of the law but had allowed their hatred and contempt for others to ferment in their hearts and spill out of their mouths. Once anger stews, it turns to bitterness. Once bitterness takes root it grows into hatred. And once hatred is allowed to grow, it may become an act of violence.

But Jesus knew that even if it never leads to violence, words can still kill. Jesus knew the power of words to heal and to harm, and He warns us about our angry words in the Sermon on the Mount: "You have heard that the law of Moses says, 'Do not murder. If you commit murder, you are subject to judgment.' But I say, if you are angry with someone, you are subject to judgment! If you call someone an idiot, you are in danger of being brought before the high council. And if you curse someone, you are in danger of the fires of hell" (Matthew 5:21–22).

Careless words spoken in haste can damage a relationship beyond repair. But more than that, they can also damage a soul beyond repair, and according to the words of our Lord, you could be guilty of violating the sixth commandment to honor life by not watching your tongue. Our tongues can be either a blessing or a curse. The choice is ours. We can choose to uplift and encourage, or we can choose to degrade, abuse, or kill with our words.

Whom in your circle of acquaintances have you hated … toward whom have you acted hatefully? Talk to God about that person today. Ask Him to forgive you of your hatred and to restore in you a heart of love.

---

1. "South Honors Fatal Culture of Violence," Cynthia Tucker, *The Atlanta-Journal Constitution*, November 28, 1999.

2. The Associated Press, "Nazis Plan to Kill Incurables to End Pain; German Religious Groups Oppose Move," *New York Times*, October 8, 1933.

9

Commandment #7
Have a Right View of Sex

Not too many years ago, a best-selling author and president of a major Christian organization was admired and respected by many believers throughout the world. While visiting a college campus to give the commencement speech, he struck up a conversation with a member of that school board. After some pleasantries, the new acquaintance asked, "If Satan were to blow you out of the water, how do you think he would do it?"

"I'm not sure I know. All sorts of ways, I suppose, but I know there's one way he wouldn't get me."

"What's that?" asked the board member.

"He'd never get me in the area of my personal relationships. That's one place where I have no doubt I'm as strong as you can get," replied the Christian leader.

Yet just a few years later, he was involved in an adulterous relationship that shattered his ministry, his marriage, and his life.[1]

This is a reminder of Satan's cunning ability to tear down and destroy the most effective Christian leaders. It is also a reminder of the weakness of our fallen flesh. That is why Paul wrote, "Let him who thinks he stands take heed that he does not fall" (1 Corinthians 10:12 NASB).

Satan knows how to use our God-given sex drives to lead us astray. He is a master manipulator whose purpose is to kill, hurt, and destroy. There is nothing he would like more than for us to violate our sacred marriage vows of fidelity.

AVOID ADULTERY, FIGHT FORNICATION

While most people consider adultery to be wrong, what about sex before marriage? People tend to view adultery and fornication as wholly distinct sins. Adultery is a sexual act with someone other than one's own spouse. Fornication, on the other hand, is an act of illicit sexual activity between unmarried persons. Thus, many people feel that they are not in violation of the seventh commandment against adultery if they commit fornication. Unfortunately, these people are splitting hairs where God sees no distinction.

While it is true that adultery and fornication represent different sins, more unites them than separates them.

In the Bible, the Greek word used for adultery, adulterer, and adulterous is *moichos*. It stands for one who has sexual intercourse with the spouse of another. Hebrews 13:4 uses the same word: "Marriage is to be held in honor among all, and the marriage bed is to be undefiled; for fornicators and adulterers God will judge" (NASB).

The Greek word used for fornicator or fornication, which denotes illicit sexual intercourse, is *porneia*. The word, which also appears in Hebrews 13:4, refers equally to immoral sexual behavior for either married or unmarried couples. Clearly, every act of adultery includes fornication. But does every act of fornication include adultery?

Note that Hebrews 13:4 refers to both "fornicators and adulterers" when issuing a command to keep the marriage bed undefiled. The point is that both fornication and adultery are outside of marriage and are therefore viewed by God as an attack upon His intended design. The intention of the seventh command-

—————❖—————

The marriage relationship serves as a picture of how much Christ loves us.

—————————

ment is to protect the institution of marriage. Fornication breaks this commandment because it is the practice of sex outside the marriage covenant. Therefore, the seventh commandment is an all-inclusive directive to avoid *all* sexual immorality, including homosexuality, lesbianism, sodomy, pornography, and any other distortion of God's sexual plan for marriage.

The seventh commandment is very simple and straightforward. It reads, "Do not commit adultery" (Exodus 20:14). No flowery words or poetry, just a clear directive from God Almighty. Do not do it. Period.

But why is God so concerned about our sexual purity? After all, He gave us our desires and passions. Why does a prohibition against marital infidelity make the top ten of moral laws? There are many reasons, but let me share several important ones with you.

IT IS A SIN AGAINST OUR BODIES

God designed us to leave our parents and cleave to one another in marriage: "As the Scriptures say, 'A man leaves his father and mother and is joined to his wife, and the two are united into one.' This is a great mystery, but it is an illustration of the way Christ and the church are one" (Ephesians 5:31–32). In marriage, this means that two people become *one flesh*. Adultery causes a severing of this one-flesh relationship, resulting in great harm to our bodies as well as our spirits.

The Bible explains why adultery is so damaging: "Don't you realize that your bodies are actually parts of Christ? Should a man take his body, which belongs to Christ, and join it to a prostitute? Never! And don't you know that if a man joins himself to a prostitute, he becomes one body with her? For as the Scriptures say, 'The two are united into one.' But the person who is joined to the Lord becomes one spirit with him. Run away from sexual sin! No other sin so clearly affects the body as this one does. For sexual immorality is sin against your own body" (1 Corinthians 6:15–18).

> *This unique physical and spiritual bond was designed by God to belong only to a husband and wife.*

To illustrate the effect of adultery upon the body, just imagine what you would have to do to give your arm to another person. Naturally, you would need to sever it from your body. In a similar way, when you give your body to another man or woman in adultery, you must sever the one-flesh relationship you share with your spouse … present or future. The Bible says that this always brings great suffering to those involved.

IT MARS MARRIAGE

Christ has made a covenant relationship with the church—a blood oath—something He will not break. That is why the church is often referred to as "the bride of Christ." Christ woos us as a man woos a woman to be His bride. He treats the church with the highest regard because it is *His* body.

Paul writes, "Husbands ought to love their wives as they love their own bodies. For a man is actually loving himself when he loves his wife. No one hates his own body but lovingly cares for it, just as Christ cares for his body, which is the church. And we are his body" (Ephesians 5:28–30).

When we treat our spouse like a prized treasure, the result is a beautiful and fulfilling marriage. This marriage relationship then serves as a picture to our children and our friends and neighbors of how much Christ loves us.

IT BRUTALLY HARMS ALL INVOLVED

Adultery does tremendous harm to a marriage. It tears husband and wife apart. To illustrate, glue two pieces of paper together. These pieces of paper represent two people who get married—they have become one. Then one spouse decides to leave the other for someone else. To show the result, pull the two pieces of paper apart. What happens? Both pieces rip and are destroyed. No matter how much care is taken in removing them from each other, they are both damaged. This is a vivid picture of the consequences of adultery.

The aftermath of adultery includes broken trust, devastating pain, divorce, and children caught in the crossfire between feuding parents! The list goes on and on from one single act of infidelity. Some of these hurts may never heal.

So we must heed the Bible's warning: Run from adultery! Flee! Do not even entertain thoughts of unfaithfulness. Although God's forgiveness will be available to anyone who repents of adultery (just as with all sins), Scripture warns that once we head down the path of sin, the consequences are inescapably destructive. This unique physical and spiritual bond was designed by God to belong only to a husband and wife. Betraying it leads to broken families, heartache, and disease.

What is there about adultery that makes so many people so susceptible? Next to eating and self-preservation, sexual desire is our strongest impulse. Most often, adultery is not just a slip-up, but a series of bad decisions that can lead to ruin. Adultery, like most sins, starts in the mind, and slowly that small voice within urges us to step just a little closer to the line until we have crossed it.

> *One of the biggest mistakes we make is to think that we are immune to adultery.*

AVOIDING ADULTERY

So what can we do to avoid entangling ourselves in this sin? Keeping in mind the following advice can help us resist temptation and remain faithful to our spouse.

GUARD THE ATTITUDE OF YOUR HEART

As with all Ten Commandments, the real issue is what goes on in our hearts. Jesus said, "You have heard that it was said, 'You shall not commit adultery'; but I say to you, that everyone who looks at a woman with lust for her has already committed adultery with her in his heart" (Matthew 5:27–28 NASB). It is our heart attitude that directs our actions. Anytime you are tempted and your heart is drawn away from your spouse, Satan is trying to influence you. Do not allow yourself to dwell on sexual thoughts that do not glorify God.

DO NOT RATIONALIZE YOUR SIN

One of the biggest mistakes we make is to think that we are immune to adultery. But given the right circumstances, we are capable of almost anything. Most adulterous relationships begin as friendships. A friendship may start as a result of one person offering comfort to someone of the opposite sex during a time of trial. Or perhaps it began due to similar interests or hobbies.

Work environments are good places for friendships to develop. Friendships are all right. The problem is when people begin to see each other in a different light. This is why it is important to create "boundaries" for ourselves to make sure that friendships remain less than intimate. Emotional attachments can quickly lead to more, especially when our needs at home are not being met.

DO NOT UNDERESTIMATE THE POWER OF YOUR SEXUALITY

We are sexual beings, so there is nothing wrong with the feelings we have. We have a deep, innate desire to procreate, and God put it there to accomplish His purpose that we "fill the earth, and subdue it" (Genesis 1:28). Sexual desires are a beautiful gift of God, but they can be distorted by Satan. Do not dismiss them. They are only evil when we dwell on them in a wrong way and eventually act upon them outside of marriage.

DO NOT DISCOUNT SATAN'S INFLUENCE

Satan knows your weaknesses and will play every trick in the book to get you to stray from your vows. But where there is temptation, there is always a way out. First Corinthians 10:13 holds the key to avoiding temptation: "Remember that the temptations that come into your life are no different from what others experience. And God is faithful. He will keep the temptation from becoming so strong that you can't stand up against it. When you are tempted, he will show you a way out so that you will not give in to it."

BEWARE OF INAPPROPRIATE RELATIONSHIPS

Because your mate knows you better than anyone else, listen when he or she warns you of an inappropriate relationship. If your wife or husband senses that a relationship you have with a person of the opposite sex is not right, end it. God gives this early warning sign to guard against adultery. Your mate's sensitivity should be one loud signal.

Another sign is if you notice that you look forward to seeing a coworker in a meeting or if you are intentionally running into a certain person to whom you are attracted. Realize the Holy Spirit is saying to you, "This could be leading to something very inappropriate." When you find yourself doing this, flee, run away, and do not look back. It will save your marriage.

LIFE APPLICATION

The seventh commandment is an all-inclusive directive to avoid all sexual immorality, including infidelity, homosexuality, sodomy, pornography, and any other distortion of God's sexual plan for marriage.

God gives us to each other in marriage to love with our whole bodies. The Bible says, "Do not deprive each other of sexual relations" (1 Corinthians 7:5). Use this gift respectfully and you will have a fruitful, loving relationship. Deny it, and one of the marriage partners will start looking for other ways to satisfy his or her deep need for intimate connection.

Listen to what Paul writes: "Husbands ought to love their

wives as they love their own bodies. For a man is actually loving himself when he loves his wife. No one hates his own body but lovingly cares for it, just as Christ cares for his body, which is the church. And we are his body" (Ephesians 5:28–30). Treating our spouse like a prized treasure can result in a beautiful and fulfilling marriage.

> *The seventh commandment is an all-inclusive directive to avoid all sexual immorality.*

God also tells us that if we simply look with lust on another person, we commit adultery in our hearts. Guard the attitude of your heart, don't rationalize your sin. Heed the warning signs about inappropriate relationships. Run from mental, emotional, and physical adultery! Scripture warns that once we head down the path of sin, the consequences are inescapable.

If you're enmeshed in some aspect of adultery, take time right now to confess your sin to God. He will forgive you. Then ask Him to heal the fracture in your marriage and to help you see what went wrong. Immediately seek counsel. A competent, trained Christian counselor can advise you on practical steps to take that will strengthen your marriage.

---

1. Gordon MacDonald, *Rebuilding Your Broken World* (Nashville, Tenn.: Nelson Books, 1988), p. 53.

———————— ❖ ————————

"You shall not steal."

EXODUS 20:15 NIV

————————————

10

Commandment #8
Respect What Belongs to Others

Many years ago after one of my lectures on being filled with the Holy Spirit, a businessman approached me and shared his deep desire to experience the wonderful blessing of the Spirit-filled life. But every time he got down on his knees to pray to be filled with the Spirit, he was convicted about what he had stolen from his employer.

I told him he really needed to confess his sin to God, then go to his employer and make restitution. He was terribly concerned that although he wanted to make things right, his employer would probably fire him. But he agreed to go.

When the man confessed his dishonesty to his employer, he was absolutely shocked by his boss' response. His boss actually congratulated him for his honesty. Then his employer offered a plan that would take a small amount of restitution from the man's paycheck each week until all had been repaid. The result was that not only did the formerly dishonest man learn a valuable lesson through paying restitution, but he subsequently experienced personally the filling (guidance, control, empowerment) of the Holy Spirit!

MIXED SIGNALS

The eighth commandment says, "Do not steal" (Exodus 20:15). Interestingly, our culture has conflicting views on the topic. People do not want others stealing from them. In that way, they favor God's law because it serves them. Legislatures allocate millions each year to make sure the eighth commandment is enforced and thieves are punished.

But other forms of stealing are considered acceptable to many. We agree that stealing someone's personal property and embezzling millions in a scam is wrong, but what about sending your insurance company an inflated claim or filing dishonest tax returns? Look at these statistics.

- Government figures show that $20 billion in taxes go uncollected every year from people who have under-reported their incomes. According to a survey done for *U.S. News & World Report*, almost a quarter of American adults cheat on their income taxes.
- The auto insurance industry reports that fraudulent claims account for as much as $20 billion each year.
- *Time* magazine reported that American workers steal $40 billion per year from their employers by doing such things as lying about their hours, making personal long-distance calls, and taking home office supplies. That sum is ten times the cost of street crime.
- Companies lose up to $350 billion annually from employees taking dishonest sick days.[1]

- In 1995, retailers lost an estimated $30 billion to theft by employees and customers. Such shoplifting increases the cost of goods by as much as 15 percent.[2]

We can see only the obvious, but God knows our hearts and requires purity even when no one is watching. Subtle, unseen dishonesty is the real test of character.

What about Christians? Do we have higher standards in our honesty? Sadly, Christians are included among these crimes. Doug Sherman and William Hendricks write in *Keeping Your Ethical Edge Sharp*, "A growing body of research suggests that religious beliefs and convictions make little difference in the behavior of people on the job."[3]

God will not be mocked.

But we often give mixed messages about honesty. A little boy got caught stealing pencils from school. When his father found out, he was enraged. He said, "Why'd you go and do something like that? If you need pencils just tell me ... I can bring some home from work."

WHY CHRISTIANS STEAL

Why do we steal, defraud, and manipulate to our advantage? I think there are two basic reasons.

A LACK OF TRUST IN GOD

God is our Provider. If we truly trust Him to meet our needs, we do not need to cut corners, withhold our due taxes from the government, or steal anything. Jesus assures us, "So don't worry about having enough food or drink or clothing. Why be like the pagans who are so deeply concerned about these things? Your heavenly Father already knows all your needs, and he will give you all you need from day to day if you live for him and make the Kingdom of God your primary concern" (Matthew 6:31–33).

A LACK OF RESPECT FOR OTHERS

Jesus said, "'You must love the Lord your God with all your heart, all your soul, and all your mind.' This is the first and greatest commandment. A second is equally important: 'Love your neighbor as yourself'" (Matthew 22:37–39). Clearly, if you love your fellow human beings as God commands, you will not steal from them.

The eighth commandment applies to strangers and extends to corporations and governmental taxing authorities. You may think these are faceless, nameless entities, but they are actually made up of people like you with families, hopes, dreams, and fears. Do not be deceived into thinking they have such deep pockets that they will not miss the little bit you defraud from them. In fact, corporations with "deep pockets" will inevitably pass losses due to dishonesty on to customers; so the damage is much more far-reaching than we'd like to think.

But most of all, God will not be mocked. His moral laws are as absolute and inviolate as the laws of physics. We will not escape God's notice if we steal in secret. Even so, many people will steal and try to cover up their theft. I once read about a developer who drained an old gravel pit before starting construction on that site. What he found was astonishing. At the bottom of the pit were a dozen almost-new cars in perfect condition. The local police traced the tags back to the owners and discovered all of them had claimed the cars had been stolen to collect on the insurance. The owners were prosecuted and jailed.

Stealing will result in consequences that by far outweigh anything one might hope to gain through the theft. Hidden sin often brings public shame.

IS THAT REALLY STEALING?

We can steal in many ways. Some are obvious, while others are not as apparent. Yet all of them are breaking God's moral laws. Let us look at several ways we steal.

BY TAKING ANYTHING THAT DOES NOT BELONG TO US

Stealing is taking anything that does not belong to you or that you did not pay for—and that includes nonmaterial things, like someone's reputation or copyrighted material. Taking the credit for someone else's work is stealing. Ordering inferior materials for a job someone is paying top dollar for is stealing. Theft comes in many forms and is always wrong. But God asks the question, "For what will it profit a man if he gains the whole world, and forfeits his soul?" (Matthew 16:26 NASB). There is nothing in this world worth gaining that interferes with our future in heaven.

BY NOT PAYING OUR BILLS

Today, people think that paying what they owe is optional in some situations. Some illegally hook up cable television in their homes, rationalizing that it hurts no one. Others run up credit-card bills and then neglect to pay when meeting the payments becomes difficult. Some allow their homes to go into foreclosure when, with sacrifice and perseverance, they could have repaid the loan. Bankruptcy and other financial loss programs were developed for people going through disastrous circumstances that cannot be solved any other way, yet these are being used more and more as quick and easy escapes from financial discomfort. As believers, we should trust God for our finances rather than defaulting on our bills.

BY NOT PAYING OUR TITHES TO GOD

God said to disobedient Israel:

> "Should people cheat God? Yet you have cheated me! But you ask, 'What do you mean? When did we ever cheat you?' You have cheated me of the tithes and offerings due to me. You are under a curse, for your whole nation has been cheating me. Bring all the tithes into the storehouse so there will be enough food in my Temple. If you do," says the LORD Almighty, "I will open the windows of heaven for you. I will pour out a blessing so great you won't have enough room to take it in! Try it! Let me prove it to you!"
>
> MALACHI 3:8–10

The word *tithe* comes from the old English word meaning "a tenth." Paying a tithe means giving one-tenth of your earned income back to God. Now someone might ask, "How can I be robbing God by not paying my tithe? It is my money."

We are stewards; God is the owner.

But the Bible teaches that God is the one who owns all the world's wealth. David declared, "The earth is the LORD's, and everything in it. The world and all its people belong to him" (Psalm 24:1).

We think we own 100 percent of our money and are giving God 10 percent in tithes. However, the truth is that God owns 100 percent of the money in our possession and claims the return of only 10 percent. We are stewards; God is the owner. Failure to pay our tithes to God is nothing less than robbery.

BY NOT WORKING AS WE SHOULD FOR OUR EMPLOYERS

The Bible says, "If you are a thief, stop stealing. Begin using your hands for honest work, and then give generously to others in need" (Ephesians 4:28).

Notice that a person is not only to steal no more, but rather is to become a hard-working employee. Why? So he can give his surplus to those who are in need. In fact, Paul writes, "Even while we were with you, we gave you this rule: 'Whoever does not work should not eat'" (2 Thessalonians 3:10).

BY OPPRESSING OUR EMPLOYEES

The eighth commandment also applies to employers. When they refuse to pay a fair wage or force their workers into longer hours for the same pay, they are guilty of theft. But the Bible promises *judgment* upon the one who oppresses his employees:

- "Then I will draw near to you for judgment ... against those who oppress the wage earner in his wages" (Malachi 3:5 NASB).
- "Do not withhold good from those to whom it is due, When it is in your power to do it" (Proverbs 3:27 NASB).
- "Scripture says, 'YOU SHALL NOT MUZZLE THE OX WHILE HE IS THRESHING,' and 'The laborer is worthy of his wages'" (1 Timothy 5:18 NASB).

What does God promise to those who deal righteously with their employees? "The generous prosper and are satisfied; those who refresh others will themselves be refreshed" (Proverbs 11:25). Paying people what they are worth and rewarding hard work pleases God. An employer will be blessed to the degree he treats his workers well.

THE SOLUTION FOR STEALING

The Gospel according to Luke says that Jesus was crucified between two criminals. While Jesus was suspended between heaven and earth in the final throes of His agony, one of the criminals said, "Are You not the Christ? Save Yourself and us!" (Luke 23:39 NASB).

But the other criminal, who was being executed as a thief, rebuked the man, saying, "Do you not even fear God, since you are under the same sentence of condemnation?" (verse 40). Then, turning to Jesus, he said, "Jesus, remember me when You come in Your kingdom!" (verse 42).

Jesus responded, "Truly I say to you, today you shall be with Me in Paradise" (verse 43).

These words, some of the very last Jesus spoke in His earthly body, demonstrate His power to forgive right up to the last seconds of His life. But what is equally interesting is that the first person to follow Christ through death and into eternity was a thief. When we put our lives in His hands, we will experience forgiveness and abundant life we do not deserve.

Jesus still forgives thieves, providing them life abundant and life eternal! There is no life so corrupt that God cannot use it. If you have a habit of stealing in some way and need forgiveness, come to Christ right now and confess your sin. God will forgive you completely. Then ask Him to begin to use you in a new and honest way to bring glory to His name. You will be amazed at what God can do with a broken vessel that is His to heal and shape. He will mold you into someone who will bring others into His kingdom!

Life Application

This commandment is pretty simple: Don't take anything that's not yours! God is our provider. And stealing shows a lack of trust in Him. Jesus assures us, "Don't worry about having enough food or drink or clothing. Why be like the pagans who are so deeply concerned about these things? Your heavenly Father already knows all your needs, and He will give you all you need from day to day if you live for Him and make the Kingdom of God your primary concern." (Matthew 6:31–33).

Subtle, unseen dishonesty is the real test of character.

We can steal in many ways. Some are obvious, while others are not as apparent. Yet all of them are breaking God's moral laws. We steal by not paying our bills; by not paying our tithes to God; by not working as fully as we should; and by oppressing our employees. Stealing is taking anything that does not belong to you or that you did not pay for—and that includes nonmaterial things like someone's reputation or credit for someone else's work.

Have you been taking something that doesn't belong to you? If you have stolen from someone, come to God right now and confess your sin. He will forgive you completely. Then ask Him to use you in a new and honest way to bring glory to His name. You will be amazed at what He can do.

1. *Moody Magazine*, July/August 1996, p. 36.

2. *U.S. News & World Report*, September 23, 1996.

3. Doug Sherman and William Hendricks, *Keeping Your Ethical Edge Sharp: How to Cultivate a Personal Character That Is Honest, Faithful, Just and Morally Clean* (Colorado Springs, Colo.: NavPress, 1990).

---❖---

"YOU SHALL NOT BEAR FALSE WITNESS
AGAINST YOUR NEIGHBOR."

EXODUS 20:16 NASB

11

Commandment #9
Tell the Truth

For many months, America and the world watched as events surrounding President Bill Clinton and White House intern Monica Lewinsky unfolded. Although almost all Americans believed Mr. Clinton's behavior was dishonest, a majority did not find the president's conduct worthy of impeachment. But among those who did believe the president had committed a removable offense, it was not his adultery but his perjury that brought to question his fitness for office.

In a CNN/USA *Today*/Gallup poll of 550 adult Americans, a significant number understood Bill Clinton lied under oath (to the question of perjury before the Starr grand jury—yes 71%, no 23%; and to the question of perjury in the Paula Jones lawsuit—yes 64%, no 27%; sampling error: +/- 5% pts). The article also reported that Clinton had "denied he committed perjury or obstruction of justice in trying to conceal their relationship." Indeed, while most Americans agreed with the House Judiciary Committee that President Bill Clinton committed perjury and abused his office, "they still [did] not want him impeached."

TELLING A LIE

The ninth commandment reads, "Do not testify falsely against your neighbor" (Exodus 20:16). Any statement that does not represent the whole truth, whether or not it harms another person, is forbidden by the ninth commandment. Not only does the ninth commandment forbid making false statements *about* our neighbor, but also statements that are made *to* our neighbor. Paul writes, "So put away all falsehood and 'tell your neighbor the truth' because we belong to each other" (Ephesians 4:25). How do we break the ninth commandment?

―――――❖―――――

The truth is, in our own wisdom, we cannot know the truth.

―――――――――

Our culture and our sinful nature both influence us to deceive ourselves and to lie. Here are a number of ways we lie: We tell little white lies; fudge the truth; tell half-truths; gossip and slander others; and say harmful words. The breakdown of truth and the ease with which so many people lie is alarming. People lie for many reasons: to be liked, to avoid punishment, or simply out of self-deception. But it is important to remember that every form of lying is hurtful.

IS IT EVER RIGHT TO LIE?

In Holland during World War II, Corrie ten Boom hid Dutch Jews in a hiding place in her family home to save them from the Nazis. If a Nazi soldier came to the door and asked her, "Are you harboring Jews in this house?" would she have been wrong to lie? Is lying always wrong? Or is it some-times justified?

What if you see a man running into an alley to escape someone who is trying to kill him and the attacker asks, "Where is he?" What would you say? Would you lie and send the attacker on a wild goose chase to protect the pursued man's life? Or would you tell the truth?

The problem addressed by the ninth commandment is the *immoral aspect* of lying.

❖

Is lying always wrong?

Although all lies are deceptive, not all deception is immoral. There are times when the dictates of morality demand we lie, as in the case of Rahab the harlot who, in faith, hid the Hebrew spies and lied concerning their whereabouts to protect them from harm. (See Joshua 2 and Hebrews 11:31.) Nonetheless, the times we are called upon to make critical decisions of this nature should be considered rare and are to be approached with much wisdom and prayer.

BREAKING FREE TO THE TRUTH

The truth is, in our own wisdom, we cannot know the truth. Our culture and our sinful nature both influence us to deceive ourselves and to lie. But we must remember who has promised to set us free. Jesus said, "You are truly my disciples if you keep obeying my teachings. And you will know the truth, and the truth will set you free" (John 8:31–32). As we focus on Jesus, who is the Truth, and on His Word, we will be able to know and reflect the truth of God. His Spirit will convict us of our lies and lead us into all truth.

LIFE APPLICATION

Any statement that does not represent the whole truth, whether or not it harms another person, is forbidden by the ninth commandment. In short, do not lie.

The right thing to do when you are tempted to embellish or change the truth is to heed Paul's counsel. He wrote, "Let no unwholesome word proceed from your mouth, but only such a word as is good for edification according to the need of the moment, so that it will give grace to those who hear" (Ephesians 4:29 NASB).

Speaking words of encouragement edifies others, and by speaking the truth in love, we help to build the body of Christ.

People lie for many reasons: to be liked, to avoid punishment, or simply out of self-deception.

Words of grace help people grow in the knowledge of Christ. They encourage others and motivate them to discover more about Christ and the abundant life He offers.

Are there times when you lie, times when you exaggerate the truth, times when you gossip? Be honest with yourself. Seek the freedom God promises. Go to Him today and ask Him to give you the freedom and power to always speak the truth. Become one who edifies others. God has promised to help you! Trust Him.

12

Commandment #10
Be Satisfied with What You Have

In his short story "The Window," author G. W. Target tells
of two seriously ill men who occupied the same hospital
room. The old man by the window was propped up for an
hour each day to drain fluid from his lungs. The younger man
spent his entire time on his back. The two men enjoyed each
other's company and talked for hours about all different types
of subjects.

During the hour he was propped up in his bed, the older
man would describe all the things he saw to his bedfast roommate, just to entertain him. Each day he would give great
detail about the activities going on outside. He described the
park with its lovely lake and grand old trees. He told of children playing and lovers walking through the park.

One day, a beautiful parade went by. Even though he
couldn't hear the music, the man on his back could see it all in
his mind as his roommate gave the details. But somehow, it
didn't seem quite fair. Although he enjoyed listening to his
friend describe the sights, he began to crave the view of his

comrade. His desire for the bed by the window became a consuming thought. It even kept him awake at night.

Then in the darkness of one sleepless night, his roommate began to cough. He was choking on the fluid in his lungs and was desperately groping for the button to call for help. The covetous roommate could have easily pushed his button to summon a nurse, but instead, he watched the old man die.

The following morning, the nurse discovered the old man's death. The standard procedure was carried out and the body was removed. The surviving man then asked that his bed be switched so he could see out the window. At last, he would have what he felt he deserved.

Painfully and slowly he struggled to prop himself up for that first look at the park. To his chagrin, the window looked out to a blank wall. The truth was his old roommate had pictured the scenes he described only in his mind. The younger man learned an important lesson: Fulfillment in life is never achieved by the venom of covetousness.

WHAT IS COVETING?

This story brings us to the tenth and final commandment, "Do not covet your neighbor's house. Do not covet your neighbor's wife, male or female servant, ox or donkey, or anything else your neighbor owns" (Exodus 20:17).

What is coveting? It means two things.

I WANT WHAT'S YOURS

Coveting is an improper craving for something another person possesses to such an extent that you cannot be happy unless you have it. It is a sinful desire for things that belong to another person.

It can be a new car your neighbor purchased. Now, there may be nothing wrong with desiring a new car. The problem comes when you desire another person's automobile.

Marriage is a wonderful gift from God. Desiring to be married is natural and God expects it. It is when you want someone else's husband or wife that you violate the tenth commandment.

I DON'T CARE WHAT GOD WANTS

The fact that we are not to covet what rightfully belongs to someone else does not mean we are free to excessively crave things that belong to no one. The tenth commandment would be violated if we were to become obsessed with sports, hobbies, or work.

> *Our principal duty is to never let our desire for things and people surpass our love for God.*

The tenth commandment clearly prohibits us from desiring to have anything that belongs to another. Nevertheless, in light of this commandment, our principal duty is to never let our desire for things and people surpass our love for God. Covetousness, in any form, turns our hearts and minds away from God as our heavenly Provider toward lusting after other things that we believe will bring joy and peace.

WHY WE COVET

It is important to understand that covetousness is an outgrowth of *greed*. Greed is an excessive appetite for possessions. Greed is a big, broad acquisitiveness that simply wants more. In the words of Henry Fairlie, "Greed loves not possessions so much as possessing. Coveting, on the other hand, is interested in one or two specific things that belong to your neighbor."

In Luke 12:15, Jesus warned against greed, saying: "Be on your guard against every form of greed; for not even when one has an abundance does his life consist of his possessions" (NASB). Here Christ's reference to "all kinds of greed" includes covetousness.

—————❖—————

Contentment means trusting God and celebrating what we have at the moment.

This is another fact: Because covetousness is an outgrowth of greed, it is not surprising that "greed" is mentioned twice as often in the Bible as "covet." God clearly wants us to avoid all kinds of greed.

One of the ways in which greed plays out in our lives is through consumer debt. The spiral of buying that has resulted from planned obsolescence has led many into debt. If that were not enough, we are constantly bombarded with advertisements that make us feel like second-rate citizens unless we have the latest thingamajig. The world we live in says, "Never be happy with what you have. Go for what you want and never mind the costs. Just keep rolling over your debt load." The result is that we have become a nation living beyond its means.

Joining the advertisers in the buying frenzy are the credit card companies. Credit cards are easily obtained and leave us virtually enslaved to the massive debt we quickly acquire. If you have good credit, you can receive an approved credit-card application each week in the mail. But the effect of "keeping up with the Joneses" has led to more covetousness and has devastated many households. Rising consumer debt is spiraling out of control for many families.

Tragically, most Christians have also accumulated too much debt. When they do, they lose their joyful freedom in serving Christ because they are worrying about how to pay their bills. Being consumed with how to meet obligations robs us of our creative energy in serving the Lord. Christ promises to meet all our needs—not our wants—according to His riches in glory. But He won't when we disobey God's commandments.

If you have too much debt, I encourage you to meet with a financial counselor who can help you set up a budget. Then, in prayer, trust God to help you be a better steward of what He has entrusted to you financially.

THE ANTIDOTE

What is the antidote to covetousness? It is contentment. And contentment is being satisfied with what you have. Once a rich industrialist was disturbed to find a fisherman sitting lazily beside his boat. "Why aren't you out there fishing?" he asked.

"Because I've caught enough fish for today," said the fisherman.

"Why don't you catch more fish than you need?" the rich man asked.

"What would I do with them?"

"You could earn more money," came the impatient reply, "and buy a better boat so you could go deeper and catch more fish. You could purchase nylon nets, catch even more fish, and make more money. Soon you'd have a fleet of boats and be rich like me."

The fisherman asked, "Then what would I do?"

"You could sit down and enjoy life," said the industrialist.

"What do you think I'm doing now?" the fisherman replied as he looked placidly out to sea.

Now there is a contented soul! However, many people are not content with what they have. To them, the grass always looks greener on the other side of the fence. These people are dissatisfied even when their circumstances are favorable and their needs are met. Instead of doing their duty cheerfully and conscientiously as unto the Lord, they yield to a spirit of covetousness. As a result, they miss God's best for their lives and fail to see the blessings God has bestowed on them.

Contentment doesn't depend on how much we have or don't have. Contentment means trusting God and celebrating what we have at the moment.

CONTENT IN EVERY CIRCUMSTANCE

In the Bible, we find a true example of contentment. As a missionary, Paul journeyed throughout the Mediterranean world. Paul's commitment to suffer for Christ and His gospel took him into extremely difficult circumstances.

In writing about his life and ministry, Paul remarks,

Five times I received from the Jews thirty-nine lashes. Three times I was beaten with rods, once I was stoned, three times I was shipwrecked, a night and a day I have spent in the deep. I have been on frequent journeys, in dangers from rivers, dangers from robbers, dangers from my countrymen, dangers from the Gentiles, dangers in the city, dangers in the wilderness, dangers on the sea, dangers among false brethren; I have been in labor and hardship, through many sleepless nights, in hunger and thirst, often without food, in cold and exposure. Apart from such external things, there is the daily pressure upon me of concern for all the churches.

2 CORINTHIANS 11:24–28 NASB

What was Paul's attitude throughout his suffering? Even when Paul's ministry landed him in a Roman prison, he found no reason to complain, but was fully content: "I know what it is to be in need, and I know what it is to have plenty. I have learned the secret of being content in any and every situation, whether well fed or hungry, whether living in plenty or in want. I can do everything through him who gives me strength" (Philippians 4:12–13 NIV). He did not have a burning desire to change his circumstances or to have more. Instead, he was content to follow God's leading in all situations.

> ❖
>
> *The tenth commandment summarizes all ten of the commandments.*

The only thing that truly satisfies is seeking Jesus Christ and His heavenly riches. Striving, coveting, and spending our time wanting what is not available to us can leave us broken and bitter. J. Paul Getty, one of the richest men who ever lived, was once asked, "How much is enough money?" His answer was, "Just a little bit more." The worst part is getting those things we wanted so badly and still feeling empty inside. The satisfaction we thought would fill us does not exist apart from Christ.

THE TENTH COMMANDMENT SUMMARIZES THE LAW

Perhaps the most outstanding aspect of the tenth commandment is that it summarizes all ten of the commandments. There is absolutely no way a person can break any one of the other nine commandments without first breaking the tenth. This same consuming covetousness is the essence of Jesus' warning, "You cannot serve God and wealth" (Luke 16:13 NASB), as well as Paul's further clarification that "the love of money is a root of all sorts of evil" (1 Timothy 6:10 NASB). Violating the tenth commandment lies at the root of all sin.

Think about it. Is it possible to tell a lie without first dishonoring your parents? Yes. Is it possible to steal without first committing adultery? Yes again. But is it possible to lie, steal, commit adultery, or even worship other gods without first being dissatisfied with your present estate? The hard answer is, no.

LIFE APPLICATION

Coveting is an inappropriate desire for something that belongs to someone else. It's craving something to such an extent that we think we can't be happy unless we have it.

Maybe it's a new car, a better home, a different job, or even what we perceive as a better marriage. There's nothing wrong with having a desire for these things. But it becomes sin when the desire develops into obsession and we want the very thing—the very car, the very home, the very job, or even the spouse—of our neighbor.

God knows us. He knows how easily we can become captivated with things we desire. When we covet we spend an inordinate amount of time and energy planning to acquire something. It means we allow our lust for material things to substitute for our true love for God. Coveting is a sinful desire for things that belong to others. If this desire is not surrendered to Christ, it will lead to outward sin, which in turn creates a snowball effect causing us to violate more of God's laws.

In light of the tenth commandment, our principle duty is never to let our desire for things and people surpass our love for God. Covetousness, in any form, turns our hearts and minds away from God as our heavenly provider.

There is only one treasure that will surpass all earthly wealth ... Christ.

The real challenge the tenth commandment lays before us is to discover there is only one treasure that will surpass all earthly wealth. That treasure is Christ. When Christ fills your heart and mind as Lord and Master, you can be at peace and content with the things, people, and circumstances God has placed in your life.

How can we defeat greed and covetousness in our lives? Through love. Love is a key principle of the covenant between God and His people. Love is about valuing a fellow human being the way God values us. To love and value another person means not taking what belongs to them, and disciplining our thought life so that we will not even think about wanting what they have.

As you pursue peace and contentment, claim for your own the words of Paul when he wrote to the Philippians: "Don't worry about anything; instead, pray about everything. Tell God what you need, and thank him for all he has done. If you do this, you will experience God's peace, which is far more wonderful than the human mind can understand. His peace will guard your hearts and minds as you live in Christ Jesus" (4:6–7).

---❖---

THE TEN COMMANDMENTS ARE NOT BURDENS;
THEY ARE LIBERATING KEYS TO LIFE.

13

Live It!

The Bible tells us that *everything* we say and do is being recorded in heaven, and that someday our "file" will be opened and we will be judged accordingly.

There is a judgment that all must face, described by John in Revelation 20:15. The all-important question at that judgment is whether one's name is "written in the book of life": that is, whether an individual has been born again.

But Paul wrote to the Corinthians of another judgment— one for believers, in which the question will not be to determine whether they will enter heaven (that "foundation," as Paul described it, has already been laid for the redeemed in Christ). The question at this point will be concerning what reward they will be given, based upon how they lived.

> For no one can lay any other foundation than the one we already have—Jesus Christ. Now anyone who builds on that foundation may use gold, silver, jewels, wood, hay, or straw. But there is going to come a time of testing at the judgment day to see what kind of work each builder has

done. Everyone's work will be put through the fire to see whether or not it keeps its value. If the work survives the fire, that builder will receive a reward. But if the work is burned up, the builder will suffer great loss. The builders themselves will be saved, but like someone escaping through a wall of flames.

1 CORINTHIANS 3:11–15

Today, many born-again believers (Paul's "builders") do not take seriously the structure they are building in life. Everyone knows you cannot build a house out of sticks and straw and hope it won't get burned when it is tested by fire. Yet when it comes to spiritual matters, many Christians disregard the consequences of their very volatile sins. But Scriptures assure believers that the consequences of sin will not only be experienced in this world—when they lie to their boss or cheat on their spouse—they will be felt as they enter eternity, too.

Up to this point, we have seen that the Ten Commandments are far more than a simple set of do's and don'ts. They are a tremendous source of peace, joy, blessing, and liberation when obeyed in the power of the Holy Spirit. But if disobeyed, the Ten Commandments become the standard God uses to judge our lives. And it is a sad scenario for some who will be saved only as one escaping through the flames, with nothing more to show for their lives.

THE PRINCIPLE OF SOWING AND REAPING

The dual ability of God's Law to act as either a source of blessings or curses is summarized by Paul in his letter to the church at Galatia. "Do not be deceived, God is not mocked; for whatever a man sows, this he will also reap. For the one who sows to his own flesh will from the flesh reap corruption, but the one who sows to the Spirit will from the Spirit reap eternal life" (Galatians 6:7–8 NASB). This is called *the principle of sowing and reaping.*

This principle comes from nature. Every year, America's farmers harvest billions of bushels of barley, corn, oats, wheat, and rye. They reap in the fall what they sowed in the spring, and, assuming proper soil and weather conditions, they reap bountifully—many times more than what was sown.

> *Many Christians disregard the consequences of their very volatile sins.*

To reap a plentiful harvest, a farmer must also be aware of the wild animals and the cunning devices they use to destroy his crop. A flock of wild ducks can strip a field of wheat in the fall, leaving only pieces of straw. Rabbits can raid a garden until all the vegetables are ruined.

In a similar way, the principle of sowing and reaping relates to every area of Christian living: If you sow adultery, you will reap a broken marriage. If you sow thievery, you will go to jail. If you sow a heart of worship to God, you will reap joy and peace. If you sow honesty, you will reap trust.

The law of sowing and reaping in our actions is as fixed as the law of gravity and as sure as the sunrise and sunset. Godly conditions govern a plentiful, spiritual harvest, and ungodly acts reap destruction and ruin.

What we do now will deeply affect our future, as Christians and certainly as non-Christians. I want to share with you five spiritual truths that will lay the all-important groundwork for you to reap a bountiful spiritual harvest.

1. TURN FROM SELF-DECEPTION

For fifteen years, Jim Fixx, author of the 1978 bestseller *The Complete Book of Running*, ran eighty miles a week. He appeared to be in tip-top shape. It did not seem possible that a man his age could be in better condition. Yet at age fifty-two, Fixx died of a massive heart attack while running alone on a Vermont road. His wife, Alice, said she was certain that Fixx had no idea he suffered from a heart problem. Why?

Jim Fixx refused to get regular checkups for fear of what they might reveal. After Fixx's death, doctors speculated that his heart muscles were so strong that he may not have felt the tell-tale chest pains or shortness of breath that usually signal arterial heart disease.

> *The Ten Commandments are not burdens; they are the liberating keys to life.*

In a similar way, many people practice avoidance in their spiritual lives. They do not want to know the real spiritual condition of their heart, so they refuse to look into God's Word to measure their behavior. They stubbornly convince themselves that as long as their actions are righteous in their own eyes, they have God's approval, which will shield them from any real consequences. This self-deception is a powerful lie.

The only solution to self-deception is to adopt a standard that is above our own ideas and thought patterns from which we can measure our thoughts and actions. When we use the Ten Commandments as our guide, we prevent ourselves from straying off a righteous path and into faulty human reasoning.

2. SEE YOUR BEHAVIOR FROM GOD'S PERSPECTIVE

Perhaps you have heard someone say in defense of sexual immorality, "What does it matter what two consenting adults do as long as they are not hurting others?" Today, people argue that because prostitution is between two consenting adults, it should not be seen differently from any other sexual act. Proponents of legalized prostitution further argue that the government can regulate prostitution and indeed profit from it through a modest tax.

What is happening here? People are attempting to erase the concept of sin from our civil laws. The victimless-crime theory totally opposes God's Word, which recognizes that such sins are an offense to God and therefore should be avoided at all costs.

Not too many years ago, our society understood that criminal acts were first sinful acts. We knew that robbing a bank or murdering a store clerk first of all violated the Law of God, then the laws of government. We also understood that even in cases where sinful acts did not bring harm or injury upon others, permitting unrestrained sin to penetrate society invites the decline of culture and the eventual downfall of a nation.

What was the basis for this understanding? Deeply embedded in our culture's consciousness was the notion that God's Law was the standard simply because it was instituted by God. What God commands is the final authority for everyone. God's Law enables us to see things from His view rather than from man's flawed reasoning.

3. Know that God Sees Everything

We often forget that God is omniscient—He knows all things.

We may be able to hide our wrongdoing from family, friends, and associates, but we can never hide it from the all-knowing, all-seeing God! He sees our sin both in the brightness of the day and in the blackness of the night, standing atop the highest mountain, or hiding beneath the sea in an underwater cave. God does see our sin—and He will repay.

4. UNDERSTAND THE LAW OF CAUSE AND EFFECT

Paul says, "The one who sows to his own flesh will from the flesh reap corruption, but the one who sows to the Spirit will from the Spirit reap eternal life" (Galatians 6:8 NASB). The law of cause and effect is one of the basic rules of life. In his teaching series entitled "Living a Life of Integrity," Reverend George Munzing says, "If you cheat in practice, you'll cheat in the game. If you cheat in your head, you'll cheat on the test. You'll cheat on the girl, you'll cheat on your mate. Compromise of God's laws leads to dishonesty in business and other similar acts. Sow a thought, reap an act. Sow an act, reap a habit. Sow a habit, reap a character. Sow a character, reap a destiny."[1]

Many people use the principle of cause and effect to their advantage in everything from business planning to how hard they should hit a tennis ball cross court. Nevertheless, many of the same people appear oblivious to how this truth relates to their relationship with God.

When God tells us that life is a series of decisions with real consequences, He is not using scare tactics, but is communicating to us the ways of life. Many seek to escape the effects of sin through trickery and deceit. But God is far wiser than that. He places the responsibility for choosing life or death squarely in our laps. The life we live is the one we wish to live—God's way or the way of death. The choice is in our own hands.

5. Look Ahead to the Final Judgment

The unassailable truth of the Bible is that someday all men, women, and children will stand before almighty God to give an account of their lives and choices. Yet people ignore this fact. While the world lives in open defiance to this truth, the attitude within the church is that a gracious God would never cause His children to stand before Him to account for their lives. But He will!

By faith, the believer must live in the full conviction that just as there is now no condemnation to those who are in Christ Jesus, we shall also all be called to account for the deeds we have performed in the flesh. Thankfully, although we will give an account for our deeds, it will be Christ's blood and righteousness that will cover the sins of His people.

Not all believers will reap the same rewards in heaven.

Don't be lulled into thinking that just because you are a believer, you will automatically earn rewards. Not all farmers reap the same-size crop. Those who work hard at sowing reap a greater harvest. Likewise, not all believers will reap the same rewards in heaven. Paul writes, "Now he who plants and he who waters are one; but each will receive his own reward according to his own labor" (1 Corinthians 3:8, NASB). We receive these rewards in relationship to the nature and the amount of good works we bring to Jesus.

To that end, if you love Jesus, then seek Him with your whole heart, mind, soul, and strength, obey His commandments, and share His gospel with others. These are the priceless gifts of good works you perform for our Lord. In return, Christ will lavish His choicest rewards upon you in glory!

The principle of sowing and reaping, then, is not a whip to keep us in line. Viewed from the platform of righteous living, it is a liberating promise to those who obey God. The Ten Commandments truly are keys that unlock blessings both now on earth and later for all eternity. They are God's gift to us, so let us practice them out of gratitude and love for our gracious heavenly Father and loving, compassionate Savior!

Many people fail to see that given the right set of circumstances, we are capable of the very things we criticize in others. The moment we feel we can understand our own inner thoughts without the illumination of God's Holy Spirit, we deceive ourselves. And in practicing self-deception, we reap a whirlwind of consequences.

The abundant life Christ offers is possible only when we are filled with the Holy Spirit and live a life of obedience and surrender. The Ten Commandments are God's gift to us, so let us practice them out of gratitude and love for our heavenly Father!

The Ten Commandments are not burdens; they are the liberating keys to life. They reveal God's love and forgiveness. They allow us to experience a relationship of love with God in its fullness. May God bless you as you walk the path of obedience to His Law in the security of His love, filled with the power of His Spirit.

---

1. George Munzing, "Living a Life of Integrity," *Preaching Today,* tape 32.

Readers' Guide

FOR PERSONAL REFLECTION
OR GROUP DISCUSSION

Q uestions are an inevitable part of life. Proud parents ask their new baby, "Can you smile?" Later they ask, "Can you say 'Mama'?" "Can you walk to Daddy?" The early school years bring the inevitable, "What did you learn at school today?" Later school years introduce tougher questions, "If X equals 12 and Y equals -14, then …?" Adulthood adds a whole new set of questions. "Should I remain single or marry?" "How did things go at the office?" "Did you get a raise?" "Should we let Susie start dating?" "Which college is right for Kyle?" "How can we possibly afford to send our kids to college?"

This book raises questions too. The following study guide is designed to (1) maximize the subject material and (2) apply biblical truth to daily life. You won't be asked to solve any algebraic problems or recall dates associated with obscure events in history, so relax. Questions asking for objective information are based solely on the text. Most questions, however, prompt you to search inside your soul, examine the circumstances that surround your life, and decide how you can best use the truths communicated in the book.

Honest answers to real issues can strengthen your faith, draw you closer to the Lord, and lead you into fuller, richer, more joyful, and productive daily adventures. So confront each question head-on and expect the One who is the answer for all of life's questions and needs to accomplish great things in your life.

Chapter 1: Find True Happiness

1. Where are many nonbelievers trying to find happiness?

2. Why is love for God the key to happiness?

3. What purpose do the Ten Commandments serve? Is it possible to keep the Ten Commandments? If so, how?

4. Why do you think so many people want to believe there is no absolute truth?

5. How are law and grace intertwined? How can God's grace enable you to observe the moral principles contained in the Ten Commandments?

Chapter 2: God's Law Leads to Christ's Grace

1. What blessings do the Ten Commandments bring to Christians?

2. How should we measure our lives—by what others do and say or by the Ten Commandments? Defend your answer.

3. What relationship, if any, do you see between God's Spirit and the Ten Commandments?

4. How would you define "cheap grace"? What kind of life results from believing in cheap grace?

5. What harm does legalism cause? How can a profound appreciation of divine grace and a desire to honor the Ten Commandments balance your life?

CHAPTER 3: KEEP GOD ABOVE ALL ELSE

1. Do you agree or disagree that Christians often try to fit God into their busy schedules rather than allowing God to plan their schedules?

2. How might your daily schedule change if you let God plan it?

3. What false gods threaten the believer's allegiance to the one true God?

4. How can believers worship God in ways that honor Him?

5. What changes will you make to strengthen your worship of God?

CHAPTER 4: SHUN IDOLS

1. How might possessions and property "destroy" a Christian?

2. In what sense is genuine worship an attitude, not an action?

3. What idols do you see Christians bowing down to? How might Christian celebrities reluctantly become idols?

4. Do you agree or disagree that covetousness is a form of idolatry? Defend your answer.

5. What steps will you take to identify idols and rid your life of them?

Chapter 5: Revere the Lord's Name

1. Does it bother you to hear God's name profaned? Why or why not?

2. Do you think too much exposure to movies and television is desensitizing Christians to the profane use of God's name? Defend your answer.

3. How does profaning God's name sully His reputation?

4. Why does wholesome speech matter?

5. How can you demonstrate to others this week that you cherish God's name?

Chapter 6: Respect the Lord's Day

1. Have you seen cultural changes in the observance of the Lord's Day? If so, what are they?

2. What biblical reasons do most Christians cite for worshiping on Sunday (the Lord's Day) rather than on Saturday (the Sabbath)?

3. Why should believers observe one day out of seven to rest and reflect?

4. How might neglecting a day of rest and reflection once a week result in personal loss?

5. How will you maximize your observance of the Lord's Day?

CHAPTER 7: HONOR YOUR PARENTS

1. What signs of disrespect of parents have you observed on the part of children? To what do you attribute this lack of respect?

2. How may adult children show proper respect for their aging parents?

3. How does respecting our parents prepare us to respect all legitimate authority?

4. If a person dies at a young age, does his early death suggest that he did not honor his parents? Why or why not?

5. What advice would you offer a believer who clashed with his or her parents and has not spoken to them for many years?

CHAPTER 8: VALUE HUMAN LIFE

1. What convictions should Christians hold regarding abortion and euthanasia? Why?

2. Should Christians support the death penalty? If so, under what circumstances should the death penalty be imposed?

3. Some people oppose the taking of life in war, claiming the sixth commandment states, "Thou shalt not kill." How would you respond to this claim?

4. How should valuing human life guide our attitudes and actions as we interact with people who represent different races, religions, and cultures? How should we relate to homosexuals?

5. How do gossip, slander, and lying contradict the belief that all human life has value? What can believers do to discourage these sins?

CHAPTER 9: HAVE A RIGHT VIEW OF SEX

1. What do you think leads to a Christian leader's moral failing? Can he or she legitimately claim, "The Devil made me do it"? Why or why not?

2. How can a congregation help its pastor maintain moral integrity?

3. Do you believe Christians can attend sexually explicit movies and not be negatively affected by the images? Why or why not?

4. What actions can believers take to be sexually pure in a culture that seems to be promiscuous?

5. How can Christian parents help their children abstain from sexual immorality?

CHAPTER 10: RESPECT WHAT BELONGS TO OTHERS

1. What do employees most often pilfer from the employers? Is it as wrong to steal inexpensive items as it is to steal expensive items? Defend your answer.

2. How has theft affected you or someone you know? How did you or the other person feel about being victimized?

3. Is it smart or criminal to cheat on an income tax return? Explain.

4. If a CEO of a corporation "cooks the books," how does that affect employees, stockholders, and society at large?

5. Do you think it would help reduce stealing if schools posted the Ten Commandments? Why or why not?

CHAPTER 11: TELL THE TRUTH

1. Do you think God considers so-called white lies as serious as other lies? Defend your answer.

2. Is telling a lie justifiable if doing so can save human life (for example, in time of war)? Defend your answer.

3. Is lying justifiable when someone compliments a person's appearance when asked for an opinion, even though he or she thinks otherwise (for example, when someone replies dishonestly, "Your new hairstyle is beautiful.")? Defend your answer.

4. In what circumstances is empty flattery a form of lying?

5. How might you encourage a believer to improve his or her ministry without lying about his or her current track record?

CHAPTER 12: BE SATISFIED WITH WHAT YOU HAVE

1. How might a poor person be more materialistic than a wealthy person?

2. What difference, if any, do you see between jealousy and envy?

3. How does slick advertising stir covetous feelings in society? How can a believer resist such advertising?

4. How can Christian parents teach their children that spiritual gain far exceeds the value of possessions and riches?

5. How can believers resist the temptation to overuse "plastic money"?

CHAPTER 13: LIVE IT!

1. What does the author identify as "the all-important question at the judgment"? Will you face this question? Why or why not?

2. If you compared the construction of your Christian ministry to the construction of a building, would it most resemble a brick, plywood, or a sticks-and-straw structure? Explain your answer.

3. Why are the Ten Commandments a good standard for judging the effectiveness of our Christian living?

4. What can a believer do to ensure a spiritual harvest?

5. How can you use the Ten Commandments as liberating keys to open your life to joy, peace, and spiritual fruitfulness?

Appendix

God's Word on Faithful Obedience

Following are selected Scripture references that were presented throughout the text of this book. We encourage you to sit down with your Bible and review these verses in their context, prayerfully reflecting upon what God's Word tells you about the joy of faithful obedience.

CHAPTER 1

Matthew 22:37–38
Romans 3:23–24

CHAPTER 2

Proverbs 1:7
John 14:21
Acts 26:20
Ephesians 2:8–10
Romans 5:8
Galatians 2:20, 21
2 Corinthians 5:21

Hebrews 6:7–8
Galatians 5:6
Deuteronomy
6:4–9
Leviticus 19:18

CHAPTER 3

Exodus 20:1–3
Deuteronomy 6:5
Psalm 139:13
Ephesians 2:10
Psalm 46:1
Mark 8:34

Matthew 6:33
Mark 12:28–30

CHAPTER 4

Exodus 20:4–6
Colossians 3:5
2 Corinthians 10:5

CHAPTER 5

Exodus 20:7
Matthew 6:9
Leviticus 22:32
Ephesians 4:25, 29

Matthew 12:34

CHAPTER 6

Exodus 20:8–11
John 20:1
Acts 2:1
Acts 20:7
Hebrews 10:25
Genesis 2:2
Genesis 1:31
1 Timothy 6:17
Mark 2:24–28
Hebrews 4:9–11,
    14

CHAPTER 7

Exodus 20:12
Deuteronomy
    21:20, 21
Romans 1:29, 30
Proverbs 10:1
Proverbs 15:5
Psalm 91:15

CHAPTER 8

Genesis 9:5–6
Exodus 21:12–22:3
Psalm 139:13–14
John 10:10

Matthew 5:21–22

CHAPTER 9

Exodus 20:13–14
1 Corinthians
    10:12–13
Hebrews 13:4
Ephesians 5:31–32
1 Corinthians
    6:15–18
Ephesians 5:28–30
1 Corinthians 7:5
Matthew 5:27–28
Genesis 1:28

CHAPTER 10

Exodus 20:15
Matthew 6:31–33
Matthew 22:37–39
Matthew 16:26
Malachi 3:8–10
Psalm 24:1
Ephesians 4:28
2 Thessalonians
    3:10
Malachi 3:5
Proverbs 3:27
1 Timothy 5:18

Proverbs 11:25
Luke 23:39–43

CHAPTER 11

Exodus 20:16
Ephesians 4:25
Joshua 2
Hebrews 11:31
John 8:31–32
Ephesians 4:29

CHAPTER 12

Exodus 20:17
Luke 12:15
2 Corinthians
    11:24–28
Philippians
    4:12–13
Luke 16:13
1 Timothy 6:10
Philippians 4:6–7

CHAPTER 13

Revelation 20:15
1 Corinthians
    3:11–15
Galatians 6:7–8
1 Corinthians 3:8

About the Author

DR. BILL BRIGHT, fueled by his passion to share the love and claims of Jesus Christ with "every living person on earth," was the founder and president of Campus Crusade for Christ. The world's largest Christian ministry, Campus Crusade serves people in 191 countries through a staff of 26,000 full-time employees and more than 225,000 trained volunteers working in some sixty targeted ministries and projects that range from military ministry to inner-city ministry.

Bill Bright was so motivated by what is known as the Great Commission, Christ's command to carry the gospel throughout the world, that in 1956 he wrote a booklet titled *The Four Spiritual Laws*, which has been printed in 200 languages and distributed to more than 2.5 billion people. Other books Bright authored include *Discover the Book God Wrote, God: Discover His Character, Come Help Change Our World, The Holy Spirit: The Key to Supernatural Living, Life Without Equal, Witnessing Without Fear, Coming Revival, Journey Home,* and *Red Sky in the Morning.*

In 1979 Bright commissioned the *JESUS* film, a feature-length dramatization of the life of Christ. To date, the film has been viewed by more than 5.7 billion people in 191 countries and has become the most widely viewed and translated film in history.

Dr. Bright died in July 2003 before the final editing of this book. But he prayed that it would leave a legacy of his love for Jesus and the power of the Holy Spirit to change lives. He is survived by his wife, Vonette; their sons and daughters-in-law; and four grandchildren.

THE LIFETIME TEACHINGS OF

Written by one of Christianity's most respected and beloved teachers, this series is a must for every believer's library. Each of the books in the series focuses on a vital aspect of a meaningful life of faith: trusting God, accepting Christ, living a spirit-filled life, intimacy with God, forgiveness, prayer, obedience, supernatural thinking, giving, and sharing Christ with others.

Dr. Bill Bright was the founder of Campus Crusade for Christ Intl., the world's largest Christian ministry. He commissioned the JESUS film, a documentary on the life of Christ that has been translated into more than 800 languages.

EACH BOOK INCLUDES A CELEBRITY-READ ABRIDGED AUDIO CD!

 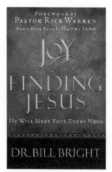 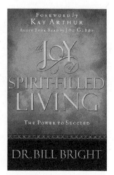

Joy of Trusting God
Foreword by Billy Graham
Audio by John Tesh
0-78144-246-X

Joy of Finding Jesus
Foreword by Pastor
Rick Warren
Audio by Naomi Judd
0-78144-247-8

Joy of Spirit-Filled Living
Foreword by Kay Arthur
Audio by Ricky Skaggs
0-78144-248-6

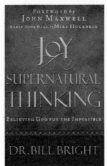
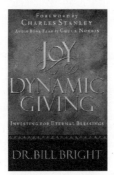

The Word at Work Around the World

A vital part of Cook Communications Ministries is our international outreach, Cook Communications Ministries International (CCMI). Your purchase of this book, and of other books and Christian-growth products from Cook, enables CCMI to provide Bibles and Christian literature to people in more than 150 languages in 65 countries.

Cook Communications Ministries is a not-for-profit, self-supporting organization. Revenues from sales of our books, Bible curricula, and other church and home products not only fund our U.S. ministry, but also fund our CCMI ministry around the world. One hundred percent of donations to CCMI go to our international literature programs.

CCMI reaches out internationally in three ways:

- Our premier International Christian Publishing Institute (ICPI) trains leaders from nationally led publishing houses around the world.

- We provide literature for pastors, evangelists, and Christian workers in their national language.

- We reach people at risk—refugees, AIDS victims, street children, and famine victims—with God's Word.

Word Power, God's Power

Faith Kidz, RiverOak, Honor, Life Journey, Victor, NexGen — every time you purchase a book produced by Cook Communications Ministries, you not only meet a vital personal need in your life or in the life of someone you love, but you're also a part of ministering to José in Colombia, Humberto in Chile, Gousa in India, or Lidiane in Brazil. You help make it possible for a pastor in China, a child in Peru, or a mother in West Africa to enjoy a life-changing book. And because you helped, children and adults around the world are learning God's Word and walking in his ways.

Thank you for your partnership in helping to disciple the world. May God bless you with the power of his Word in your life.

For more information about our international ministries, visit www.ccmi.org.